"Sara Elise has much to share about leaning into the sensate pleasures of aliveness, the fecund richness of possibility that blooms when mapping out desire paths toward a Black queer futurity that prioritizes self-worth, collectivity, nonhierarchical mindsets, access needs, care, healing, and ecological harmony. She does all of this with grace and transparency, seeding the ground for anyone who wishes to take inspiration and turn it into action. This is more than a book: It's a way of being."

—J. Wortham, culture writer for the *New York Times Magazine* and cohost of the *New York Times* podcast *Still Processing*

"Deeply honest, compassionate, and wise . . . *A Recipe for More* is a generous book about breaking cycles of suffering, but also, choosing pleasure, offering kindness to self, cultivating an electric network of friendships, and embracing this sweet life. I treasured every page."

—Janelle Monáe, singer, actor, artist, and *New York Times* bestselling author of *The Memory Librarian*

"Sara Elise's words are going to help so many people feel seen, because this book is soaked with conversations that feel like the most engaging coffee or tea date with someone who you know and can trust. By sharing her truth unapologetically, she centers experiences that invite us all to choose a more abundant life in ways that matter to us. Approachable, deep, and powerful—this book will help so many choose ease in their everyday lives."

—Yasmine Cheyenne, author of *The Sugar Jar*

A RECIPE
FOR MORE

INGREDIENTS FOR A LIFE OF ABUNDANCE AND EASE

Sara Elise

AMISTAD
An Imprint of HarperCollins*Publishers*

HarperCollins books may be purchased for educational, business, or sales promotional use. For information, please email the Special Markets Department at SPsales@harpercollins.com.

FIRST HARPERCOLLINS PAPERBACK PUBLISHED IN 2025

Designed by Janet Evans-Scanlon

Library of Congress Cataloging-in-Publication Data is available upon request.

ISBN 978-0-06-309877-0

25 26 27 28 29 LBC 5 4 3 2 1

This book is for anyone who has ever felt like they're not from this world; for people who find it difficult to live within the realms of their present embodiment and might be too sensitive for this place; for anyone who wants to see the beauty in the midst of pain and difficulty; and in the midst of hardness and the heavy, be light.

This book is for anyone who has ever hoped their softness might soften others.

CONTENTS

GRATITUDE

Thank you to those friends, lovers, ancestors, artists, creators, critics, futurists, activists, wordsmiths, disrupters, designers, and dreamers who contributed their work to this book—whether by sharing something directly with me for the purpose of writing this book or by mentioning something in passing; reading and editing my writing (and reminding me that even though it's scary, it's always best to share); philosophizing with me in cozy corners over wine; inspiring me vicariously through the way you live your life; or getting excited with me about an experience that grew us. Thank you for generously sharing yourself with me.

Origin

The most important thing each of us can know is our unique gift and how to use it in the world. Individuality is cherished and nurtured, because, in order for the whole to flourish, each of us has to be strong in who we are and carry our gifts with conviction, so they can be shared with others.

—ROBIN WALL KIMMERER, *BRAIDING SWEETGRASS*

WHEN I FIRST MET WITH MY PUBLISHING TEAM AT HARPERCOLLINS, I HAD NO idea why they had asked me to write a book. It's not that I have low self-esteem or that I don't believe my thoughts and words have value; I do. And it's not that I felt I wasn't "successful" or "well-respected" enough. At thirty-one (when I started writing this book), I had already managed to accomplish a handful of socially acclaimed things: I put myself through school and graduated from a top university, landed a coveted job in investment banking and later in private wealth management right out of business school, and pivoted careers entirely years later to create a successful sustainable catering and event design business. I have ownership in multiple real estate projects; (at the time) was in three fulfilling and supportive romantic, polyamorous relationships; am in a close-knit community of talented and thriving queer artists; have hot, kinky, and delicious sex frequently; and am a mother to a (sometimes unbearably) cute/perfect dog and around seventy-five houseplants (I am not exaggerating). And I've somehow managed to achieve all of these things in addition to a general sense of ease, joy, and well-being (which to me feels more important and by far much more interesting than all the other stuff). So by society's standards, I've made it . . .

I guess??

Still I thought, "Why *me*? What can I offer that is unique?"

I then realized that being able to achieve all the things I've just listed—especially as a Black & Indigenous, autistic, queer, femme woman with little to no familial support, or even interaction (until very recently)—while figuring out how to create a recipe for myself and my well-being that allows my life to flow and unfold and change and grow, *is* unique. And the reason I didn't at first think my story was valuable was because I hadn't encountered any books that told it. *Collins English Dictionary* says that "resistance" means the capacity to withstand something. By this definition, my very existence in this body vessel, building in these ways within the current world we live in, is in itself an act of resistance, a unique act of rebellion! And my story—the story of so many of us in oppressed communities (who are actually the majority, though often invisibilized in our work, art, and struggle) who are thinking in unconventional ways, living in response or in opposition to "the norm," withstanding the attacks and widespread disease of white toxicity and patriarchy that we all are negatively impacted by—is special. So to be able to thrive socially, emotionally, and financially despite all the external systems set up against me is inspirational, is a contribution, and is my story—which I now know is worth telling. I knew what it was like to search for my story in media and books, books that I hoped would provide connection and companionship, and not be able to find it. So I knew it was also my responsibility to share, if only so someone else might see themselves more clearly because of my self-reflection.

One of the greatest gifts in my story is being autistic; it allows me to experience life honestly. When I'm overstimulated, I need to cover my ears and remove myself to a quieter space. I often engage in body movements that release the stimulation energy that my body builds up throughout the course of the day. I move through the world with less of a social filter; I can see things as they are. As @BlairImani, one of my favorite autism spectrum disorder (ASD) Instagram advocates said, autism is "a type of neurodiversity that can be understood as different ways of thinking, processing, understanding, being, socializing, and communicating." As I've grown to understand more about how ableist the world is and how my autism is just a different but entirely valid way of existing, I've started to see how my autism has actually served as a skill set, a "special sauce." I am exceptionally good at most things that neurotypical people find difficult (like starting and running successful businesses, designing the aesthetics of a space because of my intuitive ability to read energy and notice inconsistencies, holding and sharing lots of sticky or difficult-to-communicate feelings, receiving feedback, picking up new skills very quickly) and have a lot of difficulty with things that most neurotypical people find easy (such as going to a doctor's appointment, opening containers and packages, engaging in small talk, riding the subway, talking to a new person on the phone, or dropping off a box at the post office). My brain doesn't seem to dwell long on what's socially acceptable. If I have an idea for a new business—great, let's start it. If I feel upset about something or with someone—word, let's directly communicate it. I don't seem to get caught up in the fear, initial overprocessing, and self-doubt that I watch hold many others back. Being free from these constructs has allowed me to achieve all that I have. And because I have always felt like an outsider, because I am often unable to function in the world in the way that it has been designed for others, I always consider an alternative way of being. Through that consideration, I have redesigned an alternative way of living that can work for me, largely outside of the realms of how society has dictated that I should live, so that I can enjoy my life.

Many people ask why I "don't care what people think about me," saying things like: "I love that you're so free; it's like you don't care"—which sometimes, depending on the mood I'm in, I *definitely* take as a read (eye roll). But when I asked my partner Amber why she thinks I am on the receiving end of so many messages of this kind, she broke it down for me, explaining sweetly just how powerfully my gifts apparently impact others. And I've taken the responsibility of these gifts very seriously. In fact, for me, writing this book is a way of recognizing the responsibilities that come with my gifts and valuing them enough to think that they are worthy of sharing with others. I am creating pathways of recognition for other Black and brown, queer, disabled femmes to learn about themselves. Through my work, I strive to create spaces for all people to see themselves more clearly, to identify their power(s). I hope that my very existence, out loud and unapologetic, empowers others with a permission to explore, to make changes, to play, to feel good, and to live visibly.

I also like to think of my role as an artist, and now as a writer, similarly to the way Maxine Hong Kingston talked about her role in a 1990 interview. As a Chinese woman, she questioned how society expected her to perform and the types of characters she was expected to write about. From her words, I'm encouraged to think: What if I were to disrupt your stereotypes of what you feel is acceptable for a Black autistic woman to write about? To do? Then what would happen? How do I queer even the queerest of spaces that I'm in? And when doing so, what type of space does that create or open for others? Kingston argued that it was her job as a writer to imagine a different and healthy world: "How are we going to build it if we don't imagine it?"

I think of artists and writers as first responders. Writers don't always look like we're working because a lot of our work involves slow attentiveness, gathering, and listening—making the first humble efforts. Like tulips timidly poking our heads out of the dry earth, not knowing why or what's to come but feeling something growing and changing within us that tells us it's okay to be vulnerable and also okay to be unsure—that being unsure shouldn't stop us from sprouting. Our eager buds and then eventually our bashful blooms are paving the way for the other flowers, and eventually the perennial trees, that just need a little more time, a little more assurance, one more example that it will be okay for them to also come out and play. My friend Essence, international DJ and yoga teacher, once said, "In order to normalize something, we have to be open to practicing it and sharing it." And then the streets are lined with a rich, lush abundance of green and flowering plants opening and expansive with the intoxicating scent of spring filling our lungs.

Each of us has a unique combination of skills, a unique "special sauce" that colors the way we experience the world—a unique set of gifts, beyond any projected stereotype, that can create space for others to live freely. My hope is that my sharing of my perspective will encourage you to question and cultivate (someday to perhaps even share) your own. Eventually, a positive cycle develops: our individual experience of not just surviving our lives, but *thriving* within them, grows into a collective act of enjoyment: resistance against the current systems that demand the opposite from us. This might become a new social norm, a new foundation from which we create and produce, and even an *expectation*—encouraging us all to move even just a little bit more honestly, a little bit more freely.

THIS BOOK IS FOR YOU

The day before I started writing this book, I was supposed to be filming for a crowdfunding video for Apogeo Collective, a hospitality project centering queer and trans people of color that my wife and I run together. During the filming process, I became increasingly overwhelmed. The lights were too bright; I was told to keep making direct eye contact in one place, which felt really difficult for me; with Amber and the film production company hovering around me, I felt and began to internalize my partner's nervousness; and I was utterly emotionally drained and exhausted from a stressful doctor's appointment earlier that morning. My exhaustion, coupled with what was beginning to feel like overwhelming sensory stimulation, quickly sent me into a meltdown. I had to remove myself and couldn't stop crying. I kept telling myself that I just needed to get through the day, but I couldn't pull it together enough to even go back downstairs. I spent the rest of what should have been our filming day in bed, feeling bad about wasting everyone's time, alternating between smoking weed and sleeping to self-soothe and calm my mind.

I'm sharing this with you so you know that I don't have everything figured out. I'm not writing this book because I think I have everything figured out. In fact, I am writing this book because I know that I don't. And FYI, none of us do (not even your mentor, favorite Tik Tok and Instagram influencers, or pastor—and most certainly not your parents). I have very low days and moments of self-sabotage. I have weeks where I push myself too hard and fill my schedule to the brim; moments where I deny myself pleasure or relief; days filled with overwhelming feelings of being an outsider or too different or too alone to reach out to people who I logically know care for me; times where I get lost in my fear and my anger and cannot leave the house. We are *all* limited beings. But on the days that I seem to get it right, where things click into place even just for a few moments in my mind and I feel a clarity, a lightness—I pause, and I feel my way around there *slowly*. I observe who I am and what feels true to me. I notice. I ask questions and I listen. These thoughts are just a few of the teachings that I have learned in these moments, teachings that I too am working my best to integrate in the process of sharing them with you.

As Audre Lorde said in her 1982 address for Malcolm X Weekend at Harvard University, "There are no new ideas, just new ways of giving those ideas we cherish breath and power in our own living." I am not creating the ideas in this book, as they are concepts and ideas that have been shared for generations and ones that I have learned from my friends, lovers, teachers, favorite writers, healers, mentors, and ancestors, through social media, and through medicinal-infused energetic downloads that I've received from the ether (I'm serious). And I am certainly not an expert on any of these ideas, either. I know there's so much that I am still learning every single day, after every single meltdown. I also know that the most impactful healers are the folks who are still very much committed to their own healing practice, who desire to remain students for the entirety of their lives. I know that, historically, one of the more effective ways to encourage change and growth in my communities has been through sharing and storytelling, and that the most helpful teachers realize that although each of us is the expert in our own life (the only thing we can ever truly be an expert in), each of us simultaneously always has more to learn.

This book is for you if you're committed to keeping an open perspective. If you already have an openness to change, this book can change you. If you do not, it won't. And if you're not ready to feel open, that's also okay. My hope is that you will pick up and put down this book often, coming back to it when you need it and internalizing these messages when you're receptive and ready for them.

This book is for all of us who have had to be our own teachers, our own nurturers, and sometimes even our own parents. It's for all of us who actively work to make space for our learning and our healing every day—especially if we've just gotten horrible news, thought of hurting ourselves, couldn't leave our bed, had to cancel plans because of our mental health, or had a debilitating meltdown.

Each new day is a singular moment, a singular opportunity. No day is like the last, and no day is like what's to come. In each moment, it's helpful for me to consider both that I have arrived and also that I am simultaneously arriving. I have survived and experienced so much and yet also have absolutely no clue what's in store for the rest of my time here. With this way of thinking simply, there's always room for improvement, always space to do better the next day. Space to communicate more directly with those I love. Space to forgive myself for my negative self-talk. Space to be more gentle with myself. Space for more soft-ness. My writing of this book is an encouragement to create that space—pay attention to it; pick it up in your mind's eye and hold it in your palms, see what it feels like, how light it is, how much light it radiates. If there's always space to re-create myself, always space for growth, then why do I let what has passed define my current and present choices? This book is for those of us who want to be present to the lifespace we are creating, present to what's unfolding around us, and open to the change that is possible in that empty space in each new day.

This book cannot be a space that heals you, but it can serve as a resource to help you pay attention, to be critical, to help you create more room for healing within yourself. This book can act as an invitation to both personal and collective inquiry, seeking to disrupt, to rupture—but also to balance.

EMBRACING ABUNDANCE

In simplest terms, I am writing about resistance to "what's okay" and "what's fine"; resistance to what is complacent. This book is about an embracing of an abundance mindset.

But what is an abundance mindset? What does abundance have to do with us?

Abundance is not just financial. Abundance is a vital currency for building community. Abundance does not exist solely within the self, but is a reciprocal and ongoing exchange with our community and environment. In *Braiding Sweetgrass*, Robin Wall Kimmerer says that "each person, human or no, is bound to every other in a reciprocal relationship. Just as all beings have a duty to me, I have a duty to them. If an animal gives its life to feed me, I am in turn bound to support its life. If I receive a stream's gift of pure water, then I am responsible for returning a gift in kind." Abundance is being *awake* to what's present around you. Abundance is not just something reserved for white people, men, or folks born into privileged circumstances, but is something we are all structured for. The easiest way to stop the flow of abundance is by letting ourselves be fooled into believing the harmful messaging we've received throughout our lives—messaging that causes us to doubt whether abundance is present or available for us.

An abundance mindset is a pillar of Black and Indigenous cultures. Learning that my ancestors prioritized abundance certainly changed my relationship to it, because I realized that abundance is my *birthright*; it's inherent to me and my lineage. I just needed to claim it. In fact, the "having to do the most I can do just to survive," the "having to work tirelessly to achieve just enough"—*that* is what is unnatural. The internalized oppression that leads to our disbelief that we deserve more than working nonstop just to pay for our necessities, not resting or playing or focusing on ourselves and our pleasure—this is a horribly debilitating effect of colonialism both to us as individuals and also to our collective community.

Colonialism (which is the political practice of acquiring control over an area that doesn't belong to you, occupying it with settlers, and exploiting it for economic gain), along with consequently internalized femmephobia, homophobia, transphobia, patriarchy, racism, colorism, classism, sexism, fatphobia, and ableism, is also the reason that there is power deeply entangled in whom we see as deserving of abundance, as deserving of ease, care, pleasure, and rest. I'm interested in living in a way that resists and challenges these notions.

Colonialism has us confused about how an abundance mindset differs from the ego-mind's desire for "more." But this is a very important distinction that we have to be clear on. Capitalism and the ego tell us that we always need more and that we should always strive to purchase, consume, colonize, or conquer what is outside of ourselves—that we can't possibly be happy with the items we've got, or how we look, because there's always more we should be seeking. And then this seeking, this ego-power craving, turns into an addiction that we become tethered to and cannot release. And anything we are tethered to (our phones, a person, food, alcohol, the idea of more) creates an energetic blockage or bind that stops the natural flow of energy from moving through us; it stops us from being internally free.

So how do we move away from this? How do we decolonize our thinking? Journalist Neesha Powell says that to decolonize a nonprofit means "transforming something from a site of isolation and trauma for POC employees into a space where we can find healing and liberation. Decolonizing nonprofits means decentering whiteness and honoring difference within our organizations. It means discovering how our ancestors took care of their communities before nonprofits existed and learning from their practices." But I urge us to go even further (always—don't worry, you'll get used to me doing this) than just decolonizing our nonprofits or decolonizing our workspaces. What does it look like to decolonize our families? Our home spaces? The food that we eat? Ourselves?

Why do we aim for an abundance mindset? Because the opposite of abundance is scarcity (which is actually what the ego-mind's incessant searching is rooted in)—and scarcity is the fuel of toxic capitalism and consumerism. But you might wonder how I can even begin to think about abundance when many of us are still spending so much of our time just trying to breathe, bobbing for air, flailing and drowning; or just trying to walk home with a hoodie on, or buy some cigarettes, and are literally being suffocated. How can we think about futures for marginalized people beyond surviving oppression and all that life has handed us? How can we think of creating a recipe for *more*, our recipe for *abundance*, when we always have to focus on the "lower-hanging fruit" of our survival?

My answer is this: How can we *not* think about abundance, considering the reality of the world we live in? How can we not use all of the tools that we have at our disposal in order to survive? And our imagination is just that—a tool, which we should use to imagine a future of abundance, beyond just survival, for our communities.

Poet Ross Gay responds similarly to this notion when asked by journalist and author Krista Tippett in his guest episode on her podcast *On Being*. She says, "There's a question floating around the world right now—how can we be joyful in a moment like this?" And Ross Gay responds, "How can we *not* be joyful, especially in a moment like this? It is joy by which the labor that will make the life that I want, possible. It is not at all puzzling to me that joy is possible in the midst of difficulty."

When we haven't received what we've needed our whole lives, it is natural to stay focused on just getting what we need. When we've been in danger our whole lives just by existing, it is natural to focus on protection. This is for our immediate safety and survival. As marginalized people, while focusing on the low-hanging fruit is what's natural for our survival, we also know that if we lock into that focus, then it becomes a dangerously immersive habit—and that's all that becomes of our existence. There is no room for growth or improvement there, and ultimately our focus on "just what's needed to get by" does our selves (yearning for self-actualization and fulfillment) more harm than good. We see this also in our relationships with others. A simple example: if my marriage were focused only on daily tasks that need to get done around the house—without having date nights, intimacy, freedom, playfulness, creativity, and exploration—ultimately, the relationship would suffer, because it is not growing in abundance.

And this is why I urge us all to go beyond maintaining.

A RECIPE FOR MORE

This book isn't a recipe for feeling good every single day. It's a suggestion for how to get out of your head when your head is acting as one of your main oppressors. It's a proposal to adjust our perspective to one of well-being and abundance, even when our life structures aren't set up in a way that facilitates that yet. It's about claiming abundance and pleasure and wellness as our birthright, passed down from our ancestors. This book is a meditation: a practice in remembering what we know to be true at our core even though the world tells us that we don't have the power or control over our lives. It's a call to shift our need for external approval toward remembering that we are the ones who get to validate ourselves, we are the ones who get to choose. When we remember this, we can release our self-judgment of past experiences and life choices that might be blocking us from giving ourselves the love and permission we need to grow. This book is a rumination meant to spark your imagination, but like bell hooks said, "imagination without skill is not enough," so it is also meant to serve as a resource for creating your skill set. It's about acknowledging that sometimes our usual tools, the ones we've been taught, just aren't working anymore. This book is about resistance (I mean, the book in itself is actually an act of resistance simply by existing), but more than anything, this book is a call for creativity. As activist Grace Lee Boggs highlighted in her 2012 (and very much still relevant) conversation with Dr. Angela Davis,

> *The time has come for us to reimagine everything. We have to reimagine work and go away from labor. We have to reimagine revolution and get beyond protests; we have to reimagine revolution and think not only about the changes we make to our institutions but the changes we make to ourselves. It's up to us to reimagine the alternatives and not just to protest against things and expect them to be better. . . . How do we reimagine education? How do we reimagine community? How do we reimagine family? How do we reimagine sexual identity?*

And especially in the midst of each day being both devastatingly painful and also illuminatingly beautiful, "How do we reimagine *everything*? In the light of a change that's so far-reaching, it's our responsibility to make it. We can't expect them to make it. We have to do the re-imagining ourselves."

This book is a call for imagining a future beyond anything you felt possible for yourself, which, at its core, is a creative undertaking, because creative work is not about seeing the world for how it is but imagining it for how it can be. And not seeing your life for how it is, but activating your imagination so you might see what's beyond what you've considered for yourself—the opportunities that exist even slightly outside of the sphere of normalcy that you currently experience! This book is about recognizing this imagination work, this dream work, as *necessary* work. It's about committing to the dream work in the same way you commit to your other work.

This book is rooted on the premise of the butterfly effect: the idea that a very small change in conditions can create a significantly different outcome. The idea that every Thing has the potential to touch every other Thing. The idea that simply imagining a new future for ourselves might result in even the smallest of changes in our day-to-day life, which can then ripple into something incredible, influencing ourselves and those around us in a capacity currently outside of our fantasies. That the change in our lives, small and minute in the spectrum of humanity, can create a conditional change that can impact others—the way people experience pleasure, the way people talk to one another, how patient we are with the people we love, how open our hearts are to new experiences, how free we feel.

I can imagine a world where communities are self-sustaining without the danger of corrupt and violent police, where we care for our Earth as we would a sibling or parent and allow the energy of this place to support our flow. I can imagine a world where we protect one another, where we listen to young people and value their perspectives. I can imagine us *all* prioritizing rest and play, indulging in pleasure and celebration so luscious that it drips down our chins, letting ourselves be free and full and bold and seen, using our fear and rage as tools so that each day, each singular moment, we can become better in our relationships with our selves and with our partners. I can imagine us feeling good more often than we do not—and not just "okay," but really feeling goooood. Like good good juicy good—let's all lean into this and, walls down, lean on each other good. Can you imagine this life too?

WHY A "RECIPE"?

I've been working in the food and hospitality industries for more than a decade now, but enjoying (deeply and sensuously enjoying) food for much longer than that. My enjoyment of food and curiosity of how it is grown, prepared, experienced, eaten, hoarded, and shared are things I think about often, so much so that much of how I view and live my life is centered around food and food-related experiences. This might be why I have also, since I was a young person, viewed my life in sections, or ingredients—a little bit of this and a little bit of that. Thinking of creating my life as similar in practice to cooking, or the creation of something I have agency over, is helpful framing for me. If I focus on the integrity of the recipe, making sure I stick to the fundamental structure of what I'm aiming to create, then, as with a recipe, I can take the parts that work for me, substituting out the other parts that don't. I can change the ingredients of the recipe based on the season and the space I'm creating in, paying attention to what my body needs in each moment— listening to myself and considering how things are smelling, tasting, and feeling every step of the way. Sometimes, certain ingredients work well, and other times I can't even remember why I used them. Part of the process of creating your individual recipe is about acknowledging flexibility as an underlying tool, acknowledging change as an underlying current to your human experience—and being easy, patient, flexible, and understanding with yourself when things ebb and flow along the way.

My recipe includes larger thought pillars and principles I use to guide the directional flow of my life, as opposed to having a specific set routine of day-to-day actions. I move my body very regularly, have emotionally fulfilling and connective sex often, rest *a lot*, meditate frequently, cook when I want to slow down, and spend a lot of time outside and being available to people I love. I watch the grandeur of the world with a rosy (and admittedly, maybe sometimes delusional) lens of gratitude, living (when I'm at my best) in deep attention and presence to my life, the Earth, and the people around me. All of these things add to my daily and overarching fulfillment. And then my day-to-day rituals change based on what interests me and what I need given my current intent and headspace.

Ideas are usually articulated and shared by individuals, but they're nearly almost always generated, rearranged, and put into practice by communities. My recipe is only possible because of my network of brilliant and fortifying community, friends and family and lovers, who lift me up and certainly hold me down. I am grateful for each of the contributors you will meet in this book for modeling a life of collaboration and for allowing me the chance to question and learn about myself more deeply by sharing with me an intimate access to their own lived experiences. Anaïs Nin said, "Each friend represents a world in us, a world that is possibly not born until they arrive, and it is only by this meeting that a new world is born." In each chapter, I bring in references from incredible thinkers in my community or talk to someone specifically who embodies the highlighted ingredient, someone I've learned from who has shaped the way that I think about and engage with that ingredient in my life, someone who has effectively helped emerge a new world within, and now, a part of me.

So let's (deep) dive in.

ONE

Fuck Being Busy

We are enslaved by speed and have all succumbed to the same insidious virus: Fast Life . . . May suitable doses of guaranteed sensual pleasure and slow, long-lasting enjoyment preserve us from the contagion of the multitude who mistake frenzy for efficiency.

—FOLCO PORTINARI, "THE SLOW FOOD MANIFESTO"

IN MY TWENTIES, I REALLY THOUGHT I WAS *DOING SOMETHING.* I WAS doing whatever I could to achieve the so-called success that I had been taught to aim for my entire life. I was on the "right" path: graduating with a bachelor of science from a top-tier university in Washington, DC; interning first at a well-known consumer marketing company and then on Wall Street each summer; pushing myself to double major in finance (the toughest major in business school) and marketing; cofounding networking clubs and building out my extracurriculars so that companies would be interested in hiring me, a "well-rounded young woman" (eye roll), after I finished school. Before I graduated and after countless rounds of intense interviews, I had multiple full-time offers from top consulting firms and investment banks in both DC and New York City. I ultimately chose to go to NYC, my ideal "successful businesswoman" destination, where I could clack around the marble floors of my new investment banking job in high heels, wearing pencil skirts and fitted blazers. I had big plans to head into work by 7 a.m., buckle in for a fast-paced day through 7 p.m., work out at the on-site gym while I waited for my ordered dinner to arrive, then eat and finish up work around 10 p.m. And then I would just do that every day, five to six days a week, for decades. Until (!) I became director (!) or something more important (!!) (because I was always striving to be "more important"), got a corner office, and had tons of money to separate the new me from the old me, to alert the world to my success. When I moved to Manhattan for that first job, I really thought I had made it. And here's the thing—I *had* made it in many ways. As a young, Black & Indigenous, queer woman, I was now working at a Wall Street bank and making (what I thought at the time was) big money (plus year-end bonuses) right out of college. I had to mask all day in order to engage with people in the office, but my autistic special skills, such as being able to process large amounts of information very quickly, helped get me ahead, even though I felt permanently drained. Through my job and the afterwork extracurriculars I was expected to attend, I was exposed to the wealth of NYC, and it became completely normalized for me. I was meeting "important" clients and dealing with sums of money that I had never even imagined. And also spending large sums of money to convince myself I was worthy of this new life I thought I wanted—consuming opulent dinners and never-ending cocktails; using copious amounts of drugs; impulsively taking private cars to work and eating expensive lunches; frequently getting my nails and hair done; and buying new shoes, clothes, and makeup to maintain appearances. I was purchasing and consuming many things that I didn't need in order to provide momentary dopamine rushes, because not even two years into my master success plan, I became wildly depressed.

I remember the day it all came to a breaking point. I was sitting at my computer pulling up a blank Excel workbook to begin building yet another company model from scratch, and I reached up slowly to feel dampness on my cheeks. I hadn't realized it, but I had tears streaming down my face. I sat at my desk crying, wondering where everything had gone wrong. I did everything I was told! I landed the dream job! I worked seventy-to ninety-hour weeks and had no time outside of work to do anything that I actually wanted to do. I mean, I had made my life so busy that I didn't even *know* what else I wanted to do. All I knew was that I was busy and successful, the same way everyone else there was. I had "achieved" and was doing something worth looking at, something worth celebrating (by society's standards). So why wasn't any of this adding up to fulfillment? Why did I feel so low and depleted at what was supposed to be the height of my life? This became the central question—and thankfully, because my nature is to question, everything I had built so far immediately became something worth investigating and, ultimately, tearing down.

Once I got the much coveted (and historically nearly impossible to achieve by a Black & Indigenous, openly queer woman) "seat at the table," I realized I was actually free to question whether I even wanted to sit at that table anyway. When we're always told to strive for something that we feel we can't ever reach, the act of striving becomes our destination, as if our life is in a permanent limbo of not achieving the goal, of not being good enough. But once I got there, and as I began to examine the systems that had encouraged me to get there (capitalism) and the reasons that I even felt I wanted to be part of them in the first place (social conditioning, white supremacy), I also began to interrogate myself and wondered *what was wrong with me*. The little time I wasn't spending at work, I was sleeping or drinking and doing drugs with friends. My life became a blur of loud and dark parties, nights of sleeping on friends' rooftops until the sun came up, and spontaneous hookups in party bathrooms to feel something. The only consistent staples in my kitchen were wine, olives, and frozen pizza. I had a permanent white powder spot on the dresser in my room where I would do lines nearly every day to get the energy I needed to maintain my accelerated lifestyle. I thought that I was living the dream because I could whiz through work—masking my autism the entire time, of course—to get to the few hours of "free time" I had, which I would spend numbing myself out. Because I was self-harming in ways that were socially rewarded, the damage was harder to identify at first. But because I was either masking or numbing so often during those first five years after business school, I have almost no memory of anything that happened during that time.

But what options did I have other than continuing on this path and being grateful? And where were all the parts of myself that I wasn't honoring? What did I need to tuck away and hide from (my weirdness, my autism, my queerness, my need for rest, and even sometimes my Blackness) in order to fit into this coveted world? Why was I searching for validity in a job that I wasn't even sure I wanted in the first place?

Answers came one early morning when I boarded the subway for my daily commute. Daily commutes are already stressful, but try to imagine how they feel when you're autistic. "I'm never far away from a total meltdown," Dr. Camilla Pang says about her autistic experience:

> To get an impression of how my mind works, think of the Wimbledon tennis final. The ball—my mental state—is being rallied back and forth, faster and faster. It's bouncing up and down, side to side, constantly in motion. Then, all of a sudden, there's

*a change. A player slips, makes an error or outwits their oppo-
nent. The ball spins out of control. A meltdown begins.*

So what exists for neurotypical people as a stressful commute each day represented for me—because of the crowds, the
loud noises, the uncertainty, and the bombarding smells all
leading to tons of stimulation—a daily hell.

And this morning, I was definitely not prepared to go to battle. I had been home only for around half an hour since the
night before—enough time to shower, change, and stop at the
bodega on the corner to grab a water bottle, inevitably with
some cocktail of uppers and alcohol still in my system. As I
stood in the tightly packed train car, my anxiety began bub-
bling up—from the close contact with other commuters'
morning aggressive energy, to knowing that I was about to be
late and have to engage in questioning conversation about my
arrival time with my team, to the white bright lights and
screeching train noise. I began to feel a growing panic in my
chest as my eyes started to ache and my throat started to
tighten. And then I passed out.

I woke up to people helping me sit down on a subway seat
and a kind woman offering me an orange and a granola bar.
And then it was me reassuring everyone that I was finnneeeeee,
don't worryyyyyy, and that I just had to get to work and everything would be okay. When I got to work, I debated about it for
a few hours, but then told my team that I was sick and had to go

home. That small step of self-care, that small moment when I chose myself over the illusory "dream," over the "success" that never felt like success and always felt like disconnection, discontent, and escaping from my true self, when I chose a day off instead of a day busying myself in order to not think about what was actually wrong—that small step changed everything.

I began choosing myself in small ways. I started calling out of work more (I later learned after my diagnosis that this strategy marked forms of autistic masking known as camouflaging and compensating), so that I could stay home at least one or two days a week. My mental health was still deteriorating, but I could finally see that something was very wrong. I just didn't know how to get off the hamster wheel. Jumping off without a plan seemed way too risky, and I had no clue what I actually liked to do other than drink and drug myself numb. So I picked up a hobby: I started cooking. I visited my local gardens in Bed-Stuy, Brooklyn, and started learning more about seasonal and organic ingredients that I could cook to actually help myself feel better both mentally and physically. I began to consider which decisions were ones that I was making to serve me and my future self, and which ones were just me playing "busy," making impulsive and indulgent choices that were often an impediment to my growth, leaving me anxious and stagnant. I thought a lot about how I could adjust my mindset, which had been focused on "being on the right path to success" based on what I had been told (by my parents, society, the media, and so on), to one of *Agency*. I asked myself, How can I have agency over how I feel in my body? How can I make choices that allow me to access moments of expansiveness—when I feel present, at peace, and free from (often) self-imposed constraints? How can I ease my nerves, calm my inflammation, and create a daily schedule that doesn't leave me feeling depleted and anxious each morning before the day even begins? How can I be discerning about how I spend my time—making decisions that center my future self's mental health, pleasure, and rest, rather than idolizing financial success and busyness as a marker of productivity and purpose? Instead of fighting to be somewhere that minimizes so many valid parts of me, why not create a life for myself that celebrates all that I am?

As I began cooking, I started understanding the premise of "food as medicine" and saw the changes happening in my own body and mind. My mental landscape began shifting, reshaping and reconfiguring itself to one of higher purpose. I gradually found a new focus around agency, autonomy, pleasure, and feeling well—and I wanted to share my new focus with my community. I began hosting pop-up seasonal food tasting events and eventually founded a sustainable event catering company that has provided event design and production, menu creation, and healthful meals for countless school programs, nonprofit organizations, high-fashion brand houses, galleries, private celebrity events, and corporations with ethics that we respect.

Now, more than a decade later, things are ever-changing and

ever-growing. These past couple years alone for work (in a global pandemic), Harvest & Revel Catering & Design is thriving with a new chef team and under new day-to-day management, working with large clients such as the *New York Times*, Adidas, and Peloton; Manhattan galleries like James Cohen and Hales Gallery; and with many other smaller organizations and private clients. I've modeled (with international brands such as Sephora, Bombas, and Madewell); consulted for a TV show on a major network; coached several personal clients on how to adjust their lifestyle and mindset toward one of expansiveness and abundance; launched a successful crowdfunding campaign for the QTPOC-centered hospitality project that my wife and I lead (and purchased and opened that property overseas!); participated in various paid influencer campaigns; had my writing featured in cookbooks, international newsletters, and online publications; and am writing a book (surprise!). And instead of thinking about which thing will make me the most important or successful, I let projects open, flow, and close around me based on where I feel my creativity and focus is best served. I haven't had to do anything that I don't want to do in so long, I can't even imagine what that would feel like (and honestly and only a little bit dramatically, I probably would have an adverse physical and mental reaction to putting myself in that position).

I typically work less than seven hours a week.

I realize that there is never going to be enough time in my life to do all the things that I don't want to do. I needed to move away from a mindset of time scarcity—because if I removed all the things I didn't want to do from taking up so much time, I actually had plenty of time to do everything that I did want to do. Yes, there are occasional double-bookings and moments of conflicting timing when I wish I could fit more things/activities/people I love into one day. But now the moments when I feel scheduling overwhelm are rare—and when that happens, I make sure to block out personal days on my calendar that I work hard not to compromise. For the most part, what was stressing me out was all the time that I felt I had wasted, being used for things that I didn't want to focus on, meeting up with people I didn't want to hang out with, and working on projects that I wasn't 100 percent invested in.

My life now is lucrative and *so* full, but it's not busy. I finally feel like my time is moving slowly, and that there is ample spaciousness in each day. When people ask how I've been, I never say now that "I've been busy." It's not cute to me anymore. It's not a marker for success or importance; it's a marker for constriction and mismanagement—two things that block the energetic flow of abundant energy in my life.

THE MYTH OF PRODUCTIVITY

Our culture has an addiction to "busy," an addiction to urgency. There are countless books and articles about time management and how to be more efficient so that we can accomplish and produce, produce, produce even more than we already feel pressured to produce. "Hustling," "being productive," and "grinding" are encouraged and even celebrated, while "napping," "resting," and "taking time off for myself" are either looked down on (and in particular communities, such as Black communities or mothering communities, even seen as "lazy" or "selfish") or are oddly obsessed over and revered, approached as distant goals that one can never actually achieve. When we're mentally burned out or have a physical injury or illness, the time we need to recover ("forced rest") often feels unbearable. Even when we do take consensual time off for vacation, rest, or pleasure, we often use it as a reward for our hard work and have the goal of being able to bounce back into productivity and work with even more fervor and focus upon our return. Many of us are stuck in painful cycles of working, burning out from working so much that we are forced to rest, then finally replenishing ourselves just enough so that we can work some more. Some of us even joke that our bosses "*made* us take a vacation," and many Americans don't even use all of their paid vacation days! Why?!

And have you noticed that every single one of us—when we're in this harmful cycle of toxic busyness—feels as though our work is a *very particular* and *unique* blend of important and busy that other people can't possibly understand? So we support rest for others ("Totally! Of course! You need to rest!"), but because *our* work is *very particular* and *unique*, it makes sense that we are stressed and can't take breaks and always have to work so damn hard! Why is it that each of us feels as though our distinctive work is uniquely the exception to our humanity's nature and need for rest?

When I realized that I had to step outside of my ego's desire for self-importance (that is, thinking that my work is unique, more integral, more significant) and that it's often not our actual circumstances that cause our stress, but our mindset in response to the circumstances, so much space opened up in my life. All of our work is both simultaneously majorly important and not at all important enough to risk wasting our precious time (our most limited resource) on not resting or enjoying and basking in the pleasure that this life has to offer us. But when our mindset from a young age has been programmed to prioritize efficiency, productivity, and financial success, it makes sense that we approach even our vacations and allocated time for rest with a default of busyness (and this is coming from someone who had to have a full itinerary of activities even when I was on vacation, because I couldn't sit with myself enough to simply rest in the empty space that I had intentionally carved out to do just that).

When I first quit my full-time corporate job and shifted to part-time work, I literally did not know how to spend my newly open time. I didn't know how to be alone (and especially not when I was sober). I zoomed through my days, packing them to the brim with social engagements, errands, and activities. On Sundays, I looked back at my week feeling empty and burned out (similarly to when I had worked in an office the entire week), wondering what I had actually accomplished during my busy rushing and somehow feeling that I still (despite working around fifty fewer hours per week) didn't have enough time in my day. It's only more recently that I actually feel as though time is slowing down. This past year has felt gargantuan. It's only been five months since I was last in Nicaragua hosting our latest community hospitality experience, and I feel that since then, my time has been filled with so much slowness, so much meaning, so much connection. I feel more *calm*, and as though calmness is frequently accessible and floating all around me (even in the midst of my city living).

We're not taught to develop hobbies, passions, or even a knowing of ourselves outside of our work, our production. And we are told that our producing is our most valuable way to contribute to and be included in society. Because of capitalism, we are encouraged to work until we drop, valuing external output and prioritizing that output over how we feel. Because capitalism is rooted in ego, it works best when each of us is caught in a loop of feeling as if we don't have enough—enough money, time, happiness, attention, material objects, love, acceptance. And rest is something that has been commodified, instead of just expected to be part of our natural daily cycle: It is deemed appropriate and "allowed" if we've paid for a massage or, my personal favorite, paid for a staycation (when we stay in a fancy hotel, often near our house, just so that we can give ourselves permission to fully unplug and finally rest). And because of this commodification and also systemic oppression and white supremacy, the reality is that time off, vacations, and restfulness are typically afforded most often to people with access to resources and privilege (that is, rich white people), while everyone else seems to be fighting the systems (and subsequently their own internalized oppressive mindset) for a break. So with these internalized feelings of lack, we are stuck in a loop of always wanting to *prove ourselves worthy of deserving* more, of deserving to rest.

I think about this often: What makes me feel I am undeserving of abundance, pleasure, rest, and ease?

PROVING MYSELF TO MY SELF

I ended up going to a top-tier business school and working at a Wall Street firm because I thought that's what I wanted after a lifetime of brainwashing and both explicit and implicit messaging telling me that I had to fight against being perceived as "lazy" and, especially as a Black woman, needed to always work "three times harder" than my white male counterparts to achieve the same results. I lived the majority of my life working to prove myself to a society that told me that I inherently wasn't worthy unless I was busy working, and thus I spent the majority of my life trying to prove myself to my self, hoping to get to a point *eventually* (perhaps once I achieved a director position in several years) when I might be worthy of rest and celebration—in other words, working hard enough to get to a place where I might finally enjoy my life.

In a May 2021 *Complex* magazine article, culture writer Mikeisha Dache Vaughn talks about how the concept of "grind culture" grew to be even more prevalent and celebrated *during* the global pandemic than it was previously. Now, pause for a second and think about how logically ludicrous that is. Folks all across the internet were denouncing time spent at home that was "unproductive" (translation: restful) and pushing for people to emerge from quarantine with a new business or set of skills—"comments that have flowed from a sector of Twitter users have jokingly dubbed 'Rise and Grind' and 'Grind and Hustle' Twitter. Grind culture has conditioned Black and brown people to be worker bees and feel less-than if we aren't consistently working at our 9-to-5, 24/7, and maintaining a lucrative side hustle, and right now it is vital to defer that thinking." We are exhausting ourselves, working to create output for things that *feel* crucial but are ultimately meaningless. Why?

I know what you're thinking: "Sara Elise, I need money!" And of course we all do, because we live in a capitalistic, consumer-driven society, under a corrupt government that worships billionaires, as we are engaging with media that asks us to aspire to ridiculous amounts of financial excess far beyond what any of us requires to live a comfortable life. Do we actually have use for all of the things we are being told to covet?

Do we need multiple deep freezers storing extra food, the latest iPhone every time it launches, the several different skincare routine products, the newly on-trend clothes each season, the mega-yachts? And many of us are also coming from a lineage racked with intergenerational trauma of money scarcity and shame, from people who never had access to money to get the things that they needed and who were encouraged to fight for their share to survive. But what if we think beyond our survival? When I riskily closed the door to a traditional job, I was surprised at other doors to nontraditional ways of making money that opened around me—money that changes hands within a community who loves one another, money that comes from labors of love and respect, money available to us from doing something that we might even typically be expected to do for free (such as cooking, hosting, posting on Instagram, sharing our thoughts on a podcast, making clothes, and so on).

In this achievement (and relevance) loop that we are fighting urgently to be in, we have become so disconnected from what we actually have that we are in tune only with what we don't have. We do not recognize that we are worthy simply by being. We are so "busy" striving for external gratification that we don't recognize when we actually need to focus inward to rest. We ignore the signs and end up instead with an overcommitted schedule, an emotional breakdown, or—like the celebrities of the 1990s—the need to check ourselves into a clinic for exhaustion. As an autistic person, I've noticed that I need even more rest than most other adults. A good night's slumber for me feels like getting between ten and twelve hours of sleep if I've had to engage socially that day, not including the amount of time I spend physically lying down, but not actually sleeping, during the day. And if I don't get enough rest, and this lack builds up over a period of time (could be anywhere from two days to a few weeks), my body eventually shuts down entirely, plummeting me into the depths of autism fatigue or autistic burnout. When I am fatigued, I experience extreme light sensitivity and astigmatism (so much so that I have to wear prescription light-blocking shades), sensory overload with any type of sound or smell, and an extremely debilitating migraine and body aches. All that I can do in these moments, which can last anywhere from a few hours to several days, is rest. Pushing myself to keep moving at times will literally make me so sick that my system is forced to rest.

But what if we can learn to recognize and respect our need to pause and reset *before* we experience the extreme negative effects? I'm curious about how we can use rest and pleasure as energetic fuel to get us through our day, rather than as a reward that we can access only once we've worked "enough."

One of the ways that I challenge this mindset and prioritize myself, especially when I am overwhelmed and have a lot on my plate, is by paying attention to when I begin to feel exhaustion (both physical and emotional). Some signs of my exhaustion that I'm working on noticing more readily are:

- I experience an overarching lack of fulfillment with my work—the work that I am doing feels less satisfying, and even though I am accomplishing goals I've set out for myself, I don't feel as filled by these accomplishments.

- I start to feel tired when thinking about my day or future plans; plans that I was excited for or that I would typically enjoy feel more like an obligation than a treat.

- Everything feels forced or like a struggle. When small things go wrong or there are time bottlenecks in my schedule, such as forgetting I had to walk my dog or running into a bit of traffic, I find myself feeling deeply exhausted, sad, and overwhelmed, signaling that I don't have the capacity to move through the issue with ease.

- I find it hard to regulate my emotions. Typically, I work to view my emotions as passing and without judgment, but when I'm feeling exhausted, I find that it's harder to access a logical mindset, and I am more inclined to have an emotional emergency or autistic meltdown (often over something I might typically identify as trivial if I had higher capacity).

- I feel as though I'm overcommitted to more than I can handle. I start feeling pulled in many different directions and feel as though I am holding expectations (of quality time spent together, a certain level of performance, and so on) from many different people or projects. (This is also an example of having poor boundaries.)

· I find it hard to be present and have difficulty staying focused. Attention-deficit/hyperactivity disorder (ADHD) is a comorbid diagnosis within my autism, so difficulty focusing is not new to me. But when I see an increase in that and a decrease in my ability or even in my desire to stay present, I notice that as a red flag.

When I'm recognizing these signs, I realize it's time to rest. Steph Barron Hall of NineTypes.co defines one kind of rest as solitude to recharge—but also shares that there are many other types of rest that you can give yourself permission to engage in, including time away, not being helpful, doing something unproductive, connecting to art and nature, taking a break from responsibility, being in a safe space, having alone time at home, and finding stillness to decompress.

SOLO POLYAMORY

Even if I've figured out the work balance thing, the busyness of socialization is an entirely different obstacle to tackle. Since I spend the majority of my time living in a major city surrounded by a culture of nonstop art openings, shows, parties, birthday celebrations, readings, dinners, and more, prioritizing stillness and solitude is something that I have to choose intentionally and block out as distinct time in my calendar. But solitude is one of the most important gifts we can give ourselves. We often feel we won't get invited to the next party if we aren't remembered being at the last one, or that we're pushing someone away by choosing not to spend time with them, or that we will miss an important new opportunity or miss out on deepening a connection by choosing for that moment to spend time by ourselves. Our fear of missing out and our fears of irrelevance, which are very close siblings to our fear of not being busy, are also built upon a foundation of scarcity and striving to prove ourselves—not to mention that the anxiety we feel might be a deeper reflection of an anxious attachment style. And if we want to dig even deeper (why not, right?), these fears ultimately reflect our fear of death, of not having "lived enough." I need to remind myself that connections with others will actually deepen the more I learn myself, that I will learn to love more who I am when I'm not acting in response to others at a public social event, and that saying no at times to socializing opens up necessary space for saying yes to rest and stillness. I often think about the concept of "solo polyamory," which describes the act of being in a polyamorous relationship with both yourself and others, while treating your relationship with yourself as your main focused priority. Even if you aren't polyamorous, the idea of solo polyam can teach us all lessons about what it looks like to prioritize ourselves and our well-being as the most important and significant relationship that we can nurture, one that will in turn benefit all of our other relationships as well.

The School of Life teaches that "the challenge of our lives is to learn to live deeply rather than broadly." "Fuck Being Busy" isn't about canceling everything in your life so that you can live a life of leisure, never work for money, and never have deadlines or multiple projects or feel stress ever again. But it is about being mindful of a cultural addiction to busyness that fuels a personal addiction to busyness, and challenging our internalized mindset in response to that. It's about living deeply rather than broadly.

In her book *Do Nothing*, Celeste Headlee argues that "to embrace leisure, we don't have to let go of progress. We can and must stop treating ourselves like machines that can be driven and pumped and amped and hacked. Instead of limiting and constraining our essential natures, we can celebrate our humanness at work *and* in idleness." I would even argue that stress can be helpful: it's encouraging and illuminating; it helps me figure out where I'd like to focus my energy and resources when I don't have enough time for everything and thus have to choose between tasks or priorities. But when every task on my plate is urgent, that leaves little space for imagination or creativity. We also need to recognize that the urgency, the working to "thrive under pressure" (whatever that means), the constant proving of ourselves to "stay relevant" (relevancy is not a purpose), the working to always "increase our productivity" (will productivity actually make you worthy?)—all of these mindsets have roots in capitalistic white supremacy, systems that we actively need to dismantle and resist, not feed into. Poet and founder of @NapMinistry Tricia Hersey, in her 2021 conversation with Brontë Velez, said,

> *I believe that the powers-that-be don't want us rested, they don't want the Earth rested—because they know that if folks rest enough, they're going to figure it all out. . . . Keep them numb, keep them zombies, keep them on the clock. Continue to degrade their divinity. Because once they know they're divine, they will not deal with a lot of this shit. When I say sleep helps you wake up—it helps you wake up to the fact of who the fuck you are.*

I used to get really down during winter—paralyzingly low, while experiencing debilitating mental health struggles. I thought it was seasonal depression until I realized that the season wasn't the problem. The problem was that I was forcing myself to live the same life I had been living in the spring, summer, and fall, not giving myself permission to rest, withdraw, and slow down. I was still commuting on the train to work and walking around in the cold city, trying to cram in as many social activities as I could to keep myself from the dreaded seasonal sadness. But when I realized I could actually just surrender—surrender to the change of the cycle, surrender to the slowness and the pause in the routine, giving myself permission to do fewer activities and have more rest, I began to treat winter the way the animals and plants do—as a necessary and healing part of the cycle and an excuse for giving my body and mind more of what it needs in that moment (rest).

Adopting a mindset of surrender and flow isn't about controlling external stressors that come your way, but about responding to them gently, with curiosity and intention (and attention) instead of urgency. And resting and taking care of ourselves is an active form of resistance to the systems that do not serve any of us. Paying attention to ourselves also challenges us to think about whether we're doing everything we can with our particular and peculiar set of gifts that we've been given.

What if we can invest in ourselves using rest, play, pleasure, and leisure as resources, as tools at our fingertips that will help us access more expansive, patient, and easeful parts of ourselves—and even, arguably, less busy but immensely more fulfilling parts of our lives? Instead of efficiency, what if we prioritize fulfillment? Instead of accomplishing, what if we prioritize learning, or even experience just for the sake of experiencing? What if connection was the form of currency that we valued most?

One day when I was resting on my couch scrolling through Instagram like any good millennial, I came across a page called @LivefromSnackTime, where guardians post quotes from young people expressing themselves while living their lives. There was one that stood out to me that I saved to look back at later: Charlie, three years old, said, "How about I take a nap for a treat? How about that?"

There's so much we can learn from young people always, and I was intrigued: How can we all be more like Charlie? What changes can I make right now, what actionable steps can I immediately do in my life to begin to internalize this new and brilliant way of thinking about rest that Charlie seemed to grasp innately?

So then I took a deep breath, put my phone down, and I closed my eyes.

A JOURNEY IN BLACK MINIMALISM
by Ryann Holmes

My journey in minimalism started with wanting to ease the clutter in my mind. After being inspired by Japanese minimalists such as Fumio Sasaki, author of *Goodbye, Things*, I was determined to have less. Having an excess of things I didn't use regularly took a toll on my anxiety. For example, seeing objects around my apartment would subconsciously trigger thoughts like: "I should read this book that's been sitting on the shelf for years. Why don't I read more? I'm doing a bad job and should change my lifestyle." Sounds dramatic, but the thoughts accompanying rejection sensitive dysphoria (a symptom of ADHD) can be all-consuming and take up space in your mind that could otherwise be used for dreaming, positive self-talk, and making decisions. Unbeknownst to me, owning less would be just the beginning of the journey. After downsizing my material possessions and clearing my space of extra things, I started to embody the values of minimalism in other parts of my life.

Before I get into the benefits I experienced, let's backtrack a bit. One of the most important things to figure out before committing to this practice was what my motivations were going to be. It was essential to assess my purpose. I often had to ask myself, "Why are you doing this?" The journey was so much more emotional than I was expecting. Channeling why I decided to minimize in the first place helped me set more challenging emotional boundaries— such as donating a shirt a deceased aunt gifted me, saying no to meeting up with a longtime acquaintance who drains me, and not buying things just because they are on sale.

In my journey to becoming a minimalist, it was also necessary for me to distinguish *Black* minimalism specifically from the broader concept. My perspective as a Black minimalist came from my internal observations, from reading about what other Black minimalists have experienced, and mostly from having to explain myself to other Black folks (haha!). When questioned about my motivation (or being lovingly heckled), I noticed that what was stressing Black folks out about minimalism came from many of us internalizing a scarcity mindset driven by anti-Black capitalism.

Black people have long been targets of capitalism and consumerism, which serve as barriers to creating wealth in our communities. The cycle of using our time and labor to earn money for ourselves to buy things we don't need is designed to control us. We must be wary of the traps. Consumption has become a profoundly emotional practice. We might buy things to make us feel happy, validate our individuality, or try to be someone we want to be in the future. These are not bad outcomes, but the good feelings we get are fleeting and short-term. Anti-Black capitalists work hard to market to us so that we can feel comfort and safety when we have things. We may not even need the materials we buy, but in the moment, we might confuse excess consumption with abundance. They want us to value ourselves and our success based on what we possess, and it's working. According to an article by Kori Hale in *Forbes*, "In 2019, consumer expenditures by Black households totaled approximately $835 billion, and combined spending by all Black households has increased 5 percent annually over the past two decades."

On the other hand, as a Black person, I believe in stunting and being fully expressive. That is a core pillar of Black culture that makes us beautiful, revered, and—on the downside—exploited by white people. It's even more of a staple in the Black queer community to look fly and to stunt, which may mean we have to consume things, though we've actually historically done this very well with few to no resources. The trick is not to allow material things to be all-consuming or become the foundational base of our belief systems. Objects can rule our lives, as we spend above our means to have them; pay to store them; have to spend time caring for them, cleaning them, or repairing them; and contend with the space they take up in our minds and homes. Having excess, or prioritizing consuming things that eventually leave us feeling empty or used, is detrimental to our collective well-being. We have to be careful and discerning, because excusing overconsumption can be a slippery slope.

Having *stuff* isn't the enemy, but our deeper relationship to value and the source of how we value ourselves is key to our liberation and freedom as Black folks. If you are a record collector, as I am, or a fierce Black femme who loves to accessorize (like my partner Sara Elise), you can have excess with intention, and that's still minimalism. As long as your things bring you immense joy and don't create a dynamic in which the exchange between you and the objects is unbalanced, you can experience the benefits of minimalism.

This goes for excess in so many other facets of life, too. Too much of most things can become a drain on our lives. To fully live requires living in balance. What we pour out must be replenished.

Another fact is that our sacred histories and stories as Black folks are often passed down with our hands. The truth of our legacies can be remembered by our things and the stories that live in them. Part of acknowledging this fact, but not making it a scapegoat, is about being unconventional and creative in how we preserve our heirlooms. This could look like getting rid of a dish set that was passed down through generations, but keeping a few pieces that we use as a centerpiece to decorate our space; repurposing items so that they serve us in valuable ways; making physical photo albums of select images, and scanning the rest; or giving things away to other friends or family members. Additionally, in decluttering, remember that our histories are also carried on with our voices through storytelling and that we can be even more discerning in what we choose to keep for ourselves in the physical world.

As a Black minimalist, I've committed to releasing the past and living in the present. I rarely look at old photos or spend time reminiscing. I work to let go of past relationships and moments in time that no longer serve me. I realized some of those memories are associated with past versions of myself that I have accepted but no longer identify with. I'm not saying I don't ever think of the past, but I don't live there long. My focus is on my growth and evolution of self and on supporting the people with whom I'm in active, loving relationships.

Here is a mantra on presence and looking forward:

I am present with the day and release my past. Today is a gift that I will only receive once. I will honor myself and my ancestors by living in the moment. I release all things that have happened in my past without judgment. My past memories are only stories, and the present day is my only reality.

In my journey to becoming a minimalist, I've also had to be careful about not being an extremist. Initially, my excitement and liberation from *things* blinded me to the fact that "living minimally" is just code for living intentionally. And yes, there are admittedly a few things I wish I hadn't discarded. For me, minimizing in my life has meant getting rid of shit, but also doing these things:

- Adding to my life only items that are made well (ethically) and sustainably

- Reducing my engagement with social media

- Having plans that are more occasional but higher quality

- Saving more money

- Having fewer bank and credit card accounts

- Beautifying my space

- Being more clean and tidy

- Feeling better in my space

- Feeling better in my body

- Processing more deeply

- Sleeping better

- Deepening connections with loved ones

- Communicating more thoroughly and succinctly

Being a Black nonbinary minimalist is a continuous journey; I constantly refresh my relationship with the practice. I have in no way arrived, and I welcome the ever-growing versions of myself.

Here is a journal prompt to get you started on your journey to becoming a minimalist:

1. **ASSESS YOUR PURPOSE: WHY ARE YOU DOING THIS?**

   Start decluttering your things. Make your home space a place of peace and calm.

2. **PRIORITIZE COLLECTIBLES AND DAILY/WEEKLY USE ITEMS.**

   Donate and sell as much as possible to reduce waste. (Give items to loved ones. It feels great to see people you love use things you don't need.)

3. **CREATE YOUR LIST OF VALUES AND GOALS. IF SOMETHING DOESN'T MEET THESE CRITERIA, DON'T CONSUME IT.**

What makes something a valuable contribution to your life? What are the essential qualities in an item you will bring into your life? (For example, it's well made, it's functional, it's designed in a way that brings you peace and calm, or it replaces something else that was a less good version.)

Who are the people that reflect who you are back to you (or who you aspire to grow into)?

How do you want to spend your time?

RYANN HOLMES (they/them) is a Black, queer, nonbinary person born in Washington, DC, raised in Maryland, and currently living between Brooklyn and the Catskills (with their partner Sara Elise and dog Santo). In 2009, they started the bklyn boihood (bbh) collective for Black queer and trans people to build community, tell their stories, and have safe spaces to gather. For almost two decades, bbh has been throwing legendary parties, producing photography and film projects, facilitating workshops, hosting a variety of community events, and more. Ryann is also the cofounder and artist manager at *Lucid Haus* (LH). LH is a Black and queer–led, artist-run music label that independently releases music, tours worldwide, and hosts live shows in beautiful community gardens in Brooklyn. If you'd like, you can follow Ryann on social media (though they rarely post) @supamakenzi, @bklynboihood, and @lucid.haus.

TWO

Invest in Your Pleasure

When you consider something like death, after which (there being no news flash to the contrary) we may well go out like a candle flame, then it probably doesn't matter if we try too hard, are awkward sometimes, care for one another too deeply, are excessively curious about nature, are too open to experience, enjoy a nonstop expense of the senses in an effort to know life intimately and lovingly. It probably doesn't matter if, while trying to be modest and eager watchers of life's many spectacles, we sometimes look clumsy or get dirty or ask stupid questions or reveal our ignorance or say the wrong thing or light up with wonder like the children we all are.

—DIANE ACKERMAN, *A NATURAL HISTORY OF THE SENSES*

IN FEBRUARY OF THE QUARANTINED PANDEMIC, I TOOK A VIRTUAL yoga class with my friend Essence. As we were sitting down to focus our practice, she referenced something her mentor in yoga once asked during one of their sessions together. She shared a simple question (which left my brain twisting and turning and shouting excitedly!): "Is your life turning you on?"

I think about this question often. What does it mean to live a life where I am actually and perpetually turned on? This doesn't mean that I am just out here craving sexual connection all the time—don't be basic. It means that I'm always thinking about how I can live a life that *activates* me, that encourages excitement and change and growth.

Think about how you feel when you meet a new lover you're excited about. I think often, How do I treat my life as I would a new lover? How do I create a life for myself that I want to flirt with? A life that my heart feels opened by, that causes hairs to stand up on the back of my neck, like when I'm smelling freshly baked bread? A life that makes me blush because I've once again gotten pollen underneath my nail from carefully fingering a flower (I always feel silly and a little bashful when someone points out the powdery pollen they've noticed on my nose or hands, a blatant reminder that I was indulgent past the point of practicality, intentionally ignoring my allergies for a moment of intoxicating pleasure)? How do I create a life in which I'm encouraged to be my best self because I want to impress her (my life, my ever-encouraging lover), in which I'm patient, listening, and observing because I want to learn everything about her? A life in which I'm porous and absorbent and sensitive and grounded enough to hold her changing complexities as well as my own? And how do I create a life based in profound respect of our Earth, my life's greatest foundation?

When our lives are spent seeking what makes us feel alive, the world lights up around us and in response to us. I was reminded of this a few nights ago, after a spontaneous rainy day in the city where my lover and I decided to get spicy noodles and dumplings and then end the night watching a film at the Angelika. We saw *Nine Days*, written and directed by Edson Oda, a fantasy drama film that is now on a list of my favorites. In the film, Will serves as a gatekeeper for souls, interviewing new souls (who are not yet dead or alive), for the chance to be born into a new life on Earth. Will was once alive himself and, as a soft and sensitive human, experienced much pain, heartbreak, and trauma. Because of his experience, he doesn't allow any new souls to pass who show too much of a tendency for tenderness or sensitivity, thinking that, like him in his past life, they would also be taken advantage of and experience a life of pain and heartbreak. Because of his trauma, he chooses the soul he believes has the highest chance of *survival*, with that being what he deems the main characteristic of a life well lived. But the lessons for all of us come from Emma, a questioning soul whose curiosity for life, openness to feeling, and *paying attention* forms the mindset of how she might encounter her future lived experience. When asked about her favorite moments in the human lives she was observing, unlike the others who chose "getting married" or "being at the beach," Emma was moved most by the texture of a knit blanket, the smell of pages turning in an old book, the flesh breaking and juice dripping from biting into a juicy peach. These singular moments became gifts that she took with her, forming the basis for her underlying experience of gratitude.

I wonder what our lives would look like if we were able to slow down enough to pay more attention. To fill our lives not just with large and seemingly important moments, but also with many small compilations of beauty—love notes to ourselves—until we're overwhelmed and bursting with appreciation from all that we've seen within and around us.

After the film, there was a panel, and Winston Duke, the main actor, made a guest appearance (really got to love living in NYC). When asked what he thought his personal priority would be in assessing an unborn soul's viability as a human, he said that he would choose patience as the most important characteristic: "Patience, or the capacity to develop strong patience. Patience to hurt, to heal, to make mistakes. Patience to accept the light and the dark."

Mindful indulgence in pleasure is about living a life filled with patience, because it requires us to slow down enough to see, know, and experience our pleasure—to be "mindful" of it and in it, and to "indulge" ourselves this experience. Paying attention is rooted in togetherness—you become more of what you pay attention to. If you pay attention to how grateful you are, your life becomes more steeped in gratitude. Your attentive energy attracts more of the same energy. So it's about recognizing what moments are worth paying attention to, which ones you should be spending more time with (hint: it's pretty much the opposite of what we've been taught to prioritize and value as a society). It's about discernment. It's about saying no more often, as adrienne maree brown puts it, in order to create more space for your "yes."

Considering what turns me on and activates me is one of the primary ways I think about how I'm responding to and considering pleasure. We've been taught our whole lives to have shame around accessing and receiving pleasure, so the act of prioritizing it for ourselves becomes an inherently radical act, especially if you're part of a marginalized community. In the midst of diet culture, Christina Tosi (the founder of Milk Bar) in her book *Dessert Can Save the World*, argues that "dessert is the purest road to joy and the gatekeeper to major memories. . . . These are the joy trails that begin with something sweet and lead us to the most meaningful parts of who we are and who and what we hold most precious in life. They matter because they remind us to pay attention to what kicks off joy for us—no matter how insignificant or outrageous it may seem." We need to remind ourselves simply that it is okay to indulge in the "dessert" of our lives as long as we're being mindful of how it makes our mind and body feel. It is okay to have and experience pleasure of all forms—to hold it in our bodies.

Like breath and rest and physical touch, pleasure is a basic necessity that doesn't have to be paid for with pain or parceled off in scarcity. And if your life isn't filled with enough pleasure, start filling it with more pleasure! You can always make that choice. It is *never* selfish to identify what you need and make space for it.

At university when I was discovering more about my queer-ness and Blackness, I read Audre Lorde for the first time, and she shook my world. In an effort to absorb everything, I hungrily read maybe everything she's ever published. Several years ago, my girlfriend Cristine emailed me a quote from one of Lorde's essays, "Uses of the Erotic: The Erotic as Power," as a reminder and a reference to something we had been philosophizing about:

> *This is one reason why the erotic is so feared, and so often rele-gated to the bedroom alone, when it is recognized at all. For once we begin to feel deeply all the aspects of our lives, we begin to demand from ourselves and from our life-pursuits that they feel in accordance with that joy which we know ourselves to be capable of. Our erotic knowledge empowers us, becomes a lens through which we scrutinize all aspects of our existence, forcing us to evaluate those aspects honestly in terms of their relative meaning within our lives. And this is a grave responsibility, pro-jected from within each of us, not to settle for the convenient, the shoddy, the conventionally expected, nor the merely safe.*

This has been proven true in my own life again and again. Once we open ourselves to the act of paying attention, to recognizing the miracles in each moment, we begin to build, brick by brick, a foundation of gratitude for how we experience the world. And bal-anced with that, we begin to shape forward an expectation—an expectation that keeps pushing us to envision and anticipate "the more" and not reconcile ourselves to anything less. The aspect of mindfulness also comes in here. When you are mindful of your indulgence, you are being intentional about *how much* and *what* to engage in. This mindfulness crafts the difference between indulgence as escapism (bingeing, addiction, numbing, disassociation, and procrastination), in which you lose yourself, versus indulgence as a practice that nourishes you and helps you to pay attention, helping you to *find yourself even more in your life*. You aren't settling for the convenient, but you also aren't losing yourself in mania when you find something that makes your heart sing. The goal, always, is for your balance, which will ultimately provide you with the most sustainably beneficial life experience.

WHAT IS JOY?

Sometime in the past couple of years, my close friend Naima shared with me a PDF of a letter written in 2020, seemingly exchanged between two pen pals and simply entitled "letter to julia." I think about it and have referenced it often. The letter, from poet Ica Sadagat, details her surprise in spontaneously running into her friend Julia, and her response to what must have been Julia's most recent letter, in which she asked, "What is joy to you?" Ica's short answer in thinking about joy was "inexplicable pleasure. An ecstatic emotion. A tickle, a soothe, an uplift. An embrace. Grounding. Release. Feeling found = a found feeling."

But then she shares how feeling joy can also be difficult—difficult to feel but also difficult to accept. Similarly to the way we've been conditioned to the idea of working for the reward of our rest, she thought that something could be joy only if she worked and fought hard for it. But then she realized that wasn't true. That "joy is unmissable. And it can arrive with ease." Ica shares how she is writing the letter in an exhausted state, tired from grieving and fighting and being sad, while simultaneously feeling so much gratitude for her existence, and noted how these immense and full emotions can exist at the same time, each often accompanying the other. "Part ii to [her] answer: I think joy is an invitation to be our most human selves." Joy doesn't have to come alone, but "joy is a doorway to our most human selves. our fullest selves. which is our most compassionate selves. isn't that ask glorious?"

WHAT IS PLAY?

Play is a crucial part of pleasure that a lot of adults forget to actively incorporate into our lives. Ever since one of my partners bought me the book as a gift for my twenty-ninth birthday several years ago, I think often about what Alphachanneling says in *Book of the Utopian Erotic*:

> *The real work is play! . . . When I notice dissonance, something that's feeling like work—tedious, complicated, difficult and*

tight—I ask myself: What is stopping me from feeling loose and free? What idea or expectation am I imposing on myself that is inhibiting me? . . . Why am I fighting with what I'm doing when I would prefer to be playing? When the project I'm involved with is no longer turning me on, can I revisit what was previously compelling about it, and what can I do to find myself in the center of that place again? . . . In all my creative actions, I want to be fully mindful of the spirit that is moving through me and compelling me. I want to yield to it, remain open and be present for it, and honor it with my gratitude rather than commanding, demanding and putting it to work for me. This is what I call play, the simple conscious joy of participating in the harmonic movement of life, occurring on every scale, the infinitesimal and the universal.

Play is an outlet, a portal for creativity and imagination. It's a state that allows us to heal our inner child while channeling a version of our adult selves that is more free and spontaneous and open to the world around us. Playing reminds our selves that we are safe enough in the moment to allow ourselves to experience and accept joy and pleasure.

Play is a critical part of my adult life, most actively experienced now through the practice of BDSM (bondage, discipline, sadism, and masochism). There are scenes that are constructed by both the top and the bottom that involve a consensual plan for play. There's a community that allows space for submission, dominance, make-believe, masochism, sadism, aggression, crying, laughing, intensity, tenderness, stillness, fulfillment, care, meditation—all within the realms of consent and clarity and make-believe. And it feels utterly freeing. Playing in this way with other consenting adults affirms my agency over my body—that no one has access to me or my energy without my explicit permission. In a world where I must fight for that every single day as an autistic, Black & Indigenous, queer, femme woman, this type of play allows me to create a momentary alternative universe that empowers me and reminds me that I'm in complete control. And the careful balance between play and pain I engage in through the practice of BDSM silences the movement of my overactive, overanxious mind. Because when things are feeling difficult in my mind, I crave recklessness and destruction. I sometimes argue with my partner just to hear myself argue—to funnel out restless mental energy and engage in the flashing novelty of intensity, watching myself act out another role, another version of Sara Elise (that I really don't want to feel this good portraying). But consensual and organized acts of pain-letting and play—like with boxing, or in BDSM, or running uphill on a hike until I'm gasping for air—activate that same part of my mind, the space that craves pain to fill it. I've found that the more I fill that space with choices of healthy indulgences in the parts of me that want to see how far I can push through my limits, the less I feel the need to fill the space with empty pleasures and distractions, and the less I end up unintentionally hurting myself (or others) for the sake of passion-searching.

After being raised in a very strict Baptist Christian household, I emerged into my young adulthood with the mindset that self-discipline made no sense: Why not just do what we want (play!) all of the time? At my parents' house, there were countless rules: having to have my door open at all times, not being allowed to light candles or incense, not being allowed to have sleepovers with my friends, not being allowed to shave my legs until I was sixteen, not having agency over my own body to the point that I couldn't wear certain colors of nail polish or rings or deodorant or even a bra when I felt ready to. My dad would monitor everything my siblings and I did, from printing out emails and AOL instant messages we exchanged with friends and keeping them in a folder on his desk to make sure we weren't swearing or talking about anything sexual, to installing cameras in and around the house to monitor when we left our rooms. When I made a mistake or did something outside of what they deemed "appropriate," I was dramatically punished: either physically beaten with a belt (as my dad would repeat the lesson to me while he was hitting me), "grounded" for egregious amounts of time (like the time I wasn't allowed to do any activities outside of the house, talk on the phone, watch TV, have dessert, or do anything that brought me pleasure *for six months*), or made as a child to write by hand five hundred times a Bible verse, to instill the lesson of obeying my parents. Because I came from such a controlled household where I had to follow so many rules, when I left their house to go to university

I gave myself the permission to have absolutely none. When some folks come from strict households, they tend to over-self-police, and I went the opposite route—giving myself permission to do anything I felt like doing at any time, which made it difficult to have long-lasting stable relationships, not to over-indulge in drugs and alcohol and food, not to lie, and so on. I went from wild highs to wild crashing lows, all dedicated to wanting to intensely experience the most I possibly could in every moment, because YOLO.

I don't advocate for controlling the lives of your kids (or anyone you're in relationship with) and am forever recovering from a childhood filled with intense monitoring and enforced control. But now that I have space from such an extreme version of it, I realize that self-awareness and discipline are actually the key to balance and thus the cornerstone for sustainable fulfillment and personal satisfaction: lovingly denying myself the things that are distractions from my ultimate purpose and goals provides more energy that I can direct toward those places where I do want to put my efforts. I remind myself that I can actually achieve in greater depths *even more* pleasure, fulfillment, and ultimately freedom in the areas I want, instead of wasting my energy (a limited resource) in saying yes to every whim I have.

In Sebastián Lelio's 2017 film *Disobedience*, the rabbi in the opening scene tells the story of the angel, the beast, and the human being. He says:

The angels have no will to do evil; they cannot deviate for one moment from His purpose. The beasts have only their instincts to guide them; they too follow the commands of their maker. The Torah states that Hashem spent almost six whole days of creation fashioning these creatures and then just before sunset . . . he fashioned man and woman. An afterthought, or his crowning achievement? So what is this thing—man, woman? It is a being with the power to disobey. Alone among all the creatures, we have free will. We hang suspended between the clarity of the angels and the desires of the beast. Hashem gave us "choice," which is both a privilege and a burden. We must then choose the tangled life we live.

It is not our purpose to live like either a beast with no self-discipline, torn by our instinctual whims, or an angel, following all the rules with no satisfaction of experimentation. But the ultimate gift, as well as our biggest lesson, is to take practices from both extremes to craft our decision-making, and eventually our life, to represent a balanced expression of our unique gifts and agency.

THE ART OF HOSTING

Celebration, as a momentary meditation and appreciation of togetherness, is one of my most favorite rituals to call in a mindful indulgence of pleasure. LA-based Flamingo Estate recently shared that true "hospitality" is the increasingly rare skill of making people feel transported and delighted. Through the art of hosting, I can share my hospitality with my loved ones and set the stage for just how much or how little I want my guests to experience. And the dictation doesn't need to come from controlling directly how guests participate in the space, but instead comes from what I do or do not serve for guests to consume, the type of music I play, and the types of activities I tell guests to be prepared to participate in. I love when Priya Parker, in her book *The Art of Gathering,* talks about "creating a temporary alternative world." As a host (and often with the help of creative co-hosts and collaborators), at different events I have made a tasting menu of seasonal bites for guests to enjoy while watching aerial performances; served an abundant snack spread while bringing in back-to-back DJs and asked guests to each bring a bottle of wine or mezcal; provided a seasonal brunch with an herbal tea for heart opening; served my guests kava kava root to elevate their relaxation; set up differently themed rooms (like a "Kill Room" for blood play, a medical room, and a "chapel") for BDSM play; invited my drug dealer so that everyone could purchase and take the same euphoria-enhancing drugs on-site; made and served a medicinal mushroom tea and then led a walk on the land; hosted a cacao ceremony and then led a guided dance meditation with an instrumental music producer based on the five elements; asked guests to bring snacks and aperitivo bites and provided wine and cocktails before going to a day party; and hosted a summer camp retreat where guests were prepared to play outdoor games all weekend and make s'mores by the campfire.

Each item I serve or ask guests to bring and each activity I ask guests to be prepared for is an act of intention-setting. It's a way of inviting my guests into the realms of my care and informing the shape of their experience, and our collective experience together. Through this intention-setting, I can call in the type of energy I'd like to blanket the space with, and also the energy that I want to impart on my guests when they leave. Do I want people to feel excited and manic when they go, like they had a reckless time? Do I want guests to leave feeling rooted and held by community and properly nourished? Do I want guests to leave with a deeper understanding of themselves in connection with the land? Do I want guests to feel energized to go to another event right after mine? There's a time and a space for feeling everything, and at different points of my life I have welcomed different guided intentions that are reflective of my current experience in the world. Planning is a love language of mine, a way that I can show people I am considering them so profoundly that I am planning ahead to care for and be present with them. Hosting is a way that I can put this into direct practice—planning how to "anchor my event in a meaningful purpose" (whether that's a brunch to celebrate spring, a housewarming, a retreat to rest, a party to feel outside of ourselves); sending instructions on dress and what to bring and be prepared for so that all guests can feel comfy with the amount of information they have ahead of time; planning ahead how I will welcome guests to the space (with an herbal tonic and a cooling eucalyptus washcloth, with a mezcal spritz, with a sip of Earth-medicine tea, with a warm hug); how I want the space to feel when guests arrive (What music will be playing? Will they be surrounded by fresh flowers? What type of light will there be in the space?); physically activating my space with intentional decoration (doing a floral arrangement, planning and building out the tablescape, lighting candles); considering what food and other items for consumption will be served, what activities there will be, and how I will close the event and seal the energy in the space while sending guests away with what I want them to carry home (a parting gift of incense, a cute sticker, a more grounded energy).

I think a lot about what @elviawilk said: "How do I make my entire life a love letter to my friends?" I relish in thoughts about how we can respond to beauty, joy, and pleasure in a way that preserves, celebrates, and enhances them. How do we treat each moment as a practice, a dedication to those we love? A dedication to ourselves? I've learned so much from my close friend Ora in the way she hosts and celebrates aperitivo, one of our shared Italian-heritage traditions. Aperitivo is just that, elongating a singular and arguably mundane moment (afternoon snack time) and alchemizing it into a practice of celebration—of the day, of friendship, of beauty, of hospitality, of our life, of "just because I love you."

Both hosting and attending celebrations are forms of indulging in present pleasure. I emphasize presence because, as with anything, the easiest way to experience and engage with pleasure is to give yourself permission to be present with it, regardless of the role you have in the experience. And to be present in an experience, meditation expert Tara Brach says that we must know it's happening (presence), saturate ourselves in the experience (filling ourselves up with the moment), and then appreciate it (gratitude). My favorite way of being present with pleasure is to experience things the way they're intended to be experienced when someone is thoughtful enough to have that intention for me. And when I'm having a good experience, I savor it.

Diane Ackerman, author of *A Natural History of the Senses*, says that "we are defined by how we place our attention." And to be a sensuist, she argues that "we need to return to feeling the textures of life. Much of our experience in twentieth-century America is an effort to get away from those textures, to fade into a stark, simple, solemn, puritanical, all-business routine that doesn't have anything so unseemly as sensuous zest."

You don't need to be in control of how you experience everything (as I am always reminding myself, especially as someone with diagnosed comorbid obsessive-compulsive disorder). When we're always in control, our environment is safe, yes, but also sometimes flattened and rigid, not allowing for the rich tapestry of creativity, spontaneity, and sensuality. I prefer to ask the chef how they prepare something before coming in with my idea of how I'd like it to be cooked. If you aren't always in control, you create space for trust, space for surrender—space for something joyful beyond what you might currently imagine.

A MEDITATION IN PLEASURE
by Sara Elise, Tara Aura, and J Wortham

Next time you are sitting in front of something delicious, try this practice for experiencing and receiving the present pleasures in front of you:

Allow yourself to be present with what you are about to experience, and consider that you already are experiencing it. Your journey has already begun!

What can you sense? What colors and textures are present? What do you smell?

Let yourself linger on those sensations. How—and where—do they resonate for you?

Do you breathe differently here?

Do you notice anything arising in your mind or heart center? Anticipation or excitement? Nervousness? Calm? Delight?

Now lick your lips and swallow.

Is your mouth watering? Do you feel patient? Restless? Eager?

Aroused? Breathe deeply into the sensations you feel in this moment. And for just a few more breaths, notice the container that holds your delight, and find a moment of gratitude for its beauty and the technology or ancient craftsmanship that made it a reality.

Take a bite or have a sip. Consume a part of what's in front of you.

What textures do you experience? Scratchy, smooth, slippery? Wet?

What does it feel like as it's being warmed (held? massaged?) in your mouth and is going down your throat?

Where does your tongue experience this taste most?

What does it taste like?

What elements can you recognize? Where might its ingredients come from? Imagine the land in that part of the world. Perhaps offer gratitude and thanks for the knowledge and lineages that brought this bounty to your plate.

Again, lick your lips and swallow.

Is there an aftertaste? What does it smell like now that you've held it on your tongue?

Do you breathe differently here?

What is happening in your mind? How does your heart space feel?

Notice any sounds coming from your body and give yourself permission to release any sound that wants to come out. Now begin to tune into the closest sounds you can hear as you take your next bite or sip. Take a moment to appreciate this uniquely subjective experience. Now bring your attention outside of yourself to notice:

Who is present around you, and what is their experience while you are having yours?

Does it add to your experience? Does it distract?

Do you breathe differently here?

What would it take to give yourself permission to enjoy as much as you want, whenever you want?

And finally: Do you want more?

TARA PURNELL (she/they/Tara Aura) is a meditation guide, ritual artist, certified yoga teacher, and entrepreneur who empowers people to feel better more of the time. She serves as wellness director at a progressive hotel, co-working space, and cultural institution called Eaton DC, where she produces wellness programs, events, and corporate retreats, and she also performs wellness rituals for marginalized communities as Tara Aura, cofounder of Blind Seed. With a decade of experience as a diversity, equity and inclusion facilitator, a soul singer, and a social justice advocate, Tara graduated from University of Pennsylvania's Wharton School and became a writer, multimedia producer, and brand marketing strategist before shifting her focus to health and healing arts. She has traveled the world while working in film and television and in the areas of food and beverage, fashion, tech, nonprofits, and education, but her current work centers inclusive approaches to collective care, pleasure activism, and wellness hospitality in her own hometown of Washington, DC. You can find more from her at @taraaura.

J WORTHAM (they/them) is a sound healer, breathworker, Reiki practitioner, herbalist, and community care worker oriented toward healing justice and liberation. J is the proud editor, along with Kimberly Drew, of the visual anthology *Black Futures* (One World, 2020) and is currently working on a book about the body and dissociation for Penguin Random House. They are also a staff writer for the *New York Times Magazine* and cohost of the podcast *Still Processing*.

THREE

Question Everything

What would enable us to live more porously, more mindful of the infinite changeability of our context, more open to each other and to our own needs?

—ALEXIS PAULINE GUMBS, *UNDROWNED*

PART OF BEING IN A ROMANTIC RELATIONSHIP WITH ME MEANS agreeing to a long line of questioning all the time, every day. What did you eat for breakfast? Why? How's your body feeling? What did you and your friend talk about at dinner last night? What did they order? Did you share a joint during your after-dinner walk around the neighborhood?

Having an obsessively detail-oriented brain means that information is a love language and questioning is how I express my interest. If I like you, I want to know everything about you and how you're experiencing the world. My closest friends and lovers know this and will spontaneously send me informational update texts: everything from "My work is going to be featured in a new show" and "I received some difficult news in my appointment" to "I played Bananagrams for an hour today" and "I tried a new tea today that I'm not sure I like."

I've always been extremely detail-oriented and analytical, about myself and everything happening around me. My brain feels like a baby, highly impressionable, learning quickly the new details of an ever-changing world each day, or like a sponge, rapidly seeping up the moisture of my environment—down to being able to find hair or dust particles in nearly every restaurant dish I eat and noticing immediately whether someone in the group has a slight cold that day. This compulsive obsession with detail makes me great at running businesses and hosting hospitality experiences for people, because I am able to predict how guests will experience our offerings, forecasting most potential requests and issues before they even happen. It also makes me great at designing interiors, because I am able to feel the energy of the space that I'm designing and make subtle adjustments to how things are positioned or situated in the space to impact how guests engage with the spatial layout. However, my baby sponge brain also gets very overstimulated quickly, which is why doing something that most other people can do, such as sleeping on a friend's couch for a night, is a huge "no" for me. Too many new scents and particles and hairs and hostile lighting all at one time can quickly send me into a meltdown, because when too much is displeasing or overwhelming my senses, I'm simply unable to block out the noise. (I remember when I was younger having meltdowns alone in my childhood closet, because I didn't know I was autistic and didn't feel I had an outlet, screaming and shaking and cutting myself, wondering why I was like this and what the hell I was experiencing when my mind was pulsing like a strobe light, flashing rage in front of my eyes.)

My autism diagnosis at thirty came from my compulsive questioning of everything—from knowing that there had to be an answer, or at least more information, for what I was experiencing. So much of where I am in my life today came from changes that I've made after deeply and urgently questioning something, because the biggest part of questioning everything is questioning yourself—all. the. damn. time.

adrienne maree brown wrote in a 2022 article:

if we hope to save our species, and to have human life on this planet, we have to learn from within how to live lives of satisfaction. We must practice how to move from a deep, sated, and respectful relationship to ourselves—in which we honestly articulate our needs and generate compassion for our choices—into a deep, satisfiable, and respectful relationship to anyone else.

I would argue that this journey begins with self-questioning. I'm always asking myself how I can be better—to the people I love, to the Earth we inhabit, to my self when I'm not feeling my best. And I'm also always asking myself (and thus being open to discovering) how my *life* can be better: How can I fill my life with more ease, joy, abundance, and pleasure? This practice for me has led to immense self-growth. If we walk through life with one view of ourselves, our experience becomes static and stationary. But if we're constantly questioning and "checking" ourselves, or calling ourselves out, we're committing to a daily practice of self-accountability, with a steady openness toward self-improvement. And being open to self-improvement is surely the most effective way to achieve it. To question is to consider. When we consider something, we are creating space for something, examining it, passing it back and forth between our hands, feeling it out, and getting a good look at it. Writer and speaker Brene Brown says that when we "dare to lead," we don't need to pretend to have the right answers. Instead, we must stay curious and ask the right questions.

The oppressive systems tell us to be receptive—to accept what we're given, to behave, to be polite, to be respectable and do what we're told. Questioning everything is another step to creating a life for yourself beyond the realms of these structures, beyond the realms of what other people have dreamed and decided for you. Questioning is the first step in your manifestation work, in your spell-casting. It's a process and a practice that allows you to firmly say, "I'm doing the dreaming and deciding for myself." Questioning everything is about shaking things up, shaking loose our mental bondage. Its purpose is to disrupt your patterns, patterns that usually exist not by choice but because of what you've been told and taught and thus have assumed as truth about yourself and your life path. Many of us take the same path because we believe that's the *only* path. But if we instead reclaim the agency in our choice, what could our life look like? (See Chapter 6: "Choose Who You Want to Be.") How would we live if we constantly questioned social constructs and didn't immediately internalize these made-up social rules as our truth?

Questioning everything is a ritual that allows us to approach our lives with curiosity. Curiosity imparts an open mind and an open heart with questioning that is based in information-sharing. *Collins English Dictionary* defines "curiosity" as a desire to know—whereas questioning for judgment's sake imparts criticism (of yourself and others). What does it look like to question others and yourself for the purpose of learning new information, gaining a different perspective, better understanding and more effectively providing care to yourself and others, rather than questioning for the purpose of criticizing? Questioning is about getting a snapshot of the current situation so that you can properly assess it. Only after the assessment can we determine whether changes need to be made. Questioning ourselves provides the foundation for understanding ourselves, assessing our needs, and then being able to communicate them to others. How can we expect others to love us the way that we want to be loved if we've never questioned what our needs or desires are around receiving love?

And it's important to share that the practice of questioning everything does not mean that you are perpetually dissatisfied. It means that you are committed to not being satisfied just for satisfaction's sake, that you are searching for your "yes," searching for what moves you and compels you and calls to you. And if you notice that something needs to change once you question everything, that doesn't mean that it should end or be discarded. Questioning everything is not permission for being inconsiderate, hurtful, or self-absorbed or for going only where you feel a rush of excitement and adrenaline, because then you are creating space only for addiction, numbing, and immediate satisfaction. For instance, you can spend some deep questioning time about one of your relationships and realize that you're not getting your needs met. And then you can communicate that and provide space in the relationship for things to shift over time, instead of just immediately ending the relationship. Every circumstance, along with every question, is different. And some questions are just meant to be questions, lovingly posed to yourself as a reminder or a consideration without the expectation of an answer or response.

......

RADICAL HONESTY

To that end, radical honesty should be an important aspect of your questioning practice. Radical honesty means being honest with yourself and others 100 percent of the time, even when the dishonesty might be an omission or a white lie, and even when you feel that with honesty you might hurt someone's feelings. Practicing radical honesty has freed up so much energy and space in my life, because I work to treat all information-sharing as just that—objective information-sharing—which then reduces my emotional connectivity to the information that I'm sharing or receiving. When you can treat your questioning as a means of sharing information to better yourself and everyone, rather than being tied to the outcome emotionally, the questioning (together with the information unearthed in the questioning) becomes easier to navigate. Radical honesty also encourages a more profound commitment to integrity. It encourages a more thorough thinking about consequence. If I know I am committed to being forthcoming and honest in all that I do, I'm going to do a lot less shady shit! I watch people on social media put their best face forward, always performing in alignment with how they want their brand to be perceived and as the best version of themselves because they know they're being watched. But committing to radical honesty is like agreeing to have my life be an open book, being watched and thus being accountable *all of the time*. There are no secrets (which sometimes feels sad for me because with so much Scorpio in my chart, it's true that I generally love secrets). But then with no secrets there's also no wasting energy that it takes to keep the secret, energy that could be spent creating or manifesting my life of more. This also means less drama, distrust, misunderstandings, petty arguments, feeling unsure, and increased clarity and clear communication.

Committing to radical honesty also means practicing *showing up honestly*. I didn't always view my autism as a gift. Most people who are lucky enough to receive an autism diagnosis are young white boys. Black & Indigenous women are some of the most underdiagnosed and misdiagnosed groups in the mental health field, which means that we often go through our entire lives without the language or resources that we should have to help make our lives easier and help us feel better. And even when I received my diagnosis, I had to battle internalized self-policing and ableism that at first made me feel embarrassed to have what society and doctors deem a "disorder," even though the diagnosis explained the decades of pain and the reason that, for the majority of my life, despite being surrounded by people, I have felt so crushingly alone. One of my partners started calling autism my "superpower," saying that they feel like they're dating a superhero because of all of the special gifts and abilities I have beyond those of neurotypical people, even including my compulsive questioning and analyzing. The first time I announced in public that I am autistic was at a virtual event during

COVID quarantine. I had been asked to speak on a Clubhouse panel, and many times when I'm presenting on panels or on calls, I'll encounter people experiencing me in a way that doesn't feel true to me. People will assume I'm bored or not interested because my voice is soft and mostly monotone. Or they will think that I'm standoffish or unfriendly. Or I won't laugh at the same jokes that everyone else finds funny; or people find it awkward that I get straight to the point in answering a question without padding my answers enough. When I explained this to my partner, they coached me in sharing that their colleague who has a stutter always starts her call participation by announcing that she has a stutter. They said, "Why not announce your difference so as to give folks the opportunity to receive you openly?" This allows other participants to know what to expect and creates an open space for folks to not make immediate judgments. If they still do, that's on them. Sharing also offers me an opportunity to enter a space honestly, without demanding of myself that I "mask" to hide my differences.

Autistic masking is the process of minimizing or altering one's natural autistic characteristics and behaviors in an effort to appear "less autistic," to fit in with social norms or what we perceive as a neurotypical environment. Many of us mask socially to some extent in different situations, such as when we are at work as opposed to when we are with our family or people we feel comfortable around. But for autistics, masks are not convenient or light to wear. Someone once compared autistic masking to having to wear high heels. If every time you leave the house and interact with others, you are expected to wear heels, you might be fine for the first few hours. But in time, wearing heels during all of your social interactions starts to hurt your back, your knees, and your feet. As you look around at everyone else wearing comfortable sneakers, you frequently wonder why you're the only one who didn't get the memo about wearing the "correct" footwear and why you're the only person who seems uncomfortable, but you don't own any sneakers, anyway. After a while, you're so exhausted by having to engage socially through the intensifying discomfort that you can't even stand, but everyone else seems energized and is going on a hike. You join them so that you feel included and connected, but eventually you need to go home because the pain and exhaustion are just too unbearable.

Sometimes, however, I do want to wear heels, to add more height or to feel fancier or to infuse more femme energy into my look. Masking can also be used as an intentional tool by many autistics; we can use it to connect with others, infuse a certain energy into the social interaction, or even to feel safe in social situations where we don't want to explain that we are autistic. Writer Akwaeke Emezi wrote in their book *Pet* that "masks [are] useful . . . not quite lies, not quite truths. Just decisions about what to be and what to show. Curation." But I don't want to feel that I need to wear heels, or my mask, all the time. And sometimes I just don't have the energetic capacity to mask, since masking for autistics can be extremely energy-consuming and lead to autistic burnout, when I experience such deep fatigue that it's hard for me to leave my bed.

No one listening to a panel of speakers would want a speaker with a stutter to feel strain, shame, and exhaustion trying to change how they naturally speak. We all want the people in our community to be encouraged, embraced, and known for exactly who they are. It's hard work to maneuver through my internalized ableism, but I am gradually accepting that no one would want me to be anyone but myself, either. And that when I show up honestly, it also welcomes others to stop pretending. Before the panel call, I had my usual debilitating social anxiety (which I have for every event, whether I'm presenting or sitting in the audience), and then during my introduction, I said, "Hi, my name is Sara Elise, my pronouns are she/her, and I'm autistic." This was a small moment in naming myself, but after making the announcement, I broke down crying, and my entire body was shaking. It felt like such a groundbreaking moment to announce myself, even if just to a group of thirty virtual guests, most of whom I didn't know.

Practicing radical honesty, like questioning everything, is first about being honest with yourself. Once I developed an honest relationship with myself, which meant seeing and accepting myself *fully* (see Chapter 4: "Let Yourself Be Visible"), it made being honest with others that much more crucial. I can't have integrity with my thoughts and words if the words I'm communicating to others aren't true. I can't have integrity with how I'm living my life if I'm living it in the shadows because of self-judgment or internalized ableism. The process of radical honesty within your questioning practice allows everyone to move the way they need to once we all have full information. These care practices help us all to determine what we need to love ourselves and those around us more effectively.

GIVE YOURSELF PERMISSION TO CHANGE

Sometimes, questioning ourselves leads to answers in the form of new pathways and major life pivots. Allow yourself (and others) this change. And remember, it is not your responsibility to be an older version of yourself just because people around you are more comfortable with that version. If people are not open to your changing, then they do not have to be in your life anymore. And no, I'm not advocating for discarding people every time you're going through major changes, but ask yourself: Do you feel loved and supported by this person? After spending time together, do you leave feeling inspired or energized or more fulfilled? It's always useful and important to assess each person's contribution to your energy.

My autism diagnosis in my thirties answered a lifetime of questions for me, but it also sparked a deeper level of questioning around aspects of myself that I *thought* I knew to be true. I used to identify as a party kid, going out three to four times a week, meeting several new people each night, thinking that I craved the intensity of loud music and piercing lights through the cover of darkness. It was only a few years ago that I realized how completely intoxicated I needed to be in order to numb myself enough to have fun in these environments. Yes, I did like the loud music, but I had to drink eight cocktails first to dull my senses enough to the stimulation to actually be able to be present with the music. And then, as was true for much of my numbed-out twenties, I'd forget about the experience a few weeks later anyway.

I've always said that I felt lucky that I didn't get easily addicted to any of the substances I was liberally consuming, but I now realize I was addicted to the numbing. I was addicted to the adrenaline rush that came from the stress my mind was experiencing in response to the overstimulation. My favorite combination of "helpers" was a particular mix of cocaine, alcohol, and Xanax, which provided enough of an upper to keep me energized and not drained from all the social interaction, but also enough anti-anxiety effects to take the edge off my nerves. This was a complete "*fuck you*" to my brain, which was trying to situate itself in the middle of both extremes and would eventually just tap out, leading to me blacking or browning out the entire evening, even when I wasn't drowning in alcohol.

Now, I'm able to identify what I actually enjoy, what I can experience pleasurably without having to first numb myself into complete disconnection of my senses in order to be present with it. I'm finding excitement in more calm and less stimulating environments, and allowing myself to shift out of how I once identified.

With my diagnosis as the prompt, I was able to deeper dive into my truth seeking. Once we're able to actually identify what works for us, we must give ourselves permission to pivot, even when there are still people who want to party with us, who are used to us being a way that works for them, who might not understand our changing. Give yourself permission to say what's true for you out loud, to turn down the events (and company) your nervous system doesn't feel good around. Release older versions of you that are no longer true or, upon further investigation, appear to have been untrue all along.

It's also important to allow other people to change the way they show up in your life if the way they are changing feels in alignment with the life you are creating for yourself. My parents had me when they were teenagers, and I grew up in a household where they were grasping for control and stability. My young mom, anxious and overwhelmed, once told me that she didn't like me or enjoy spending time with me. I've committed to countless hours of self-work to heal from their parenting, to learn to stop seeking love externally that I would later find within myself. And now my mom is in a much better place and making a recognized and real effort in my life: showing up in Brooklyn to visit me and play games in the park with my family here, sharing online articles about autism that she finds useful, and spending weekends with me and my partner at our home in Upstate, New York. I tentatively (and still with boundaries) am accepting our changing relationship and opening to the learning and love evolving between us.

WHAT IS EVERYTHING?

"Everything" is every force at work in your life. It might be obvious to question a romantic partner or a job; those forces confront us in direct ways every single day. But when I say "question everything," I ask you to consider the forces that are less obvious as well. A friendship that is merely "tolerable" to you, the way you speak to yourself when you look into the mirror, the lyrics in the music you listen to, the images you watch on-screen—how does each single force produce a butterfly effect in the way you value yourself and your time, respect others, care for our Earth, distract you from your focused goals, resign to a mindset of martyrdom, or harm your self-esteem? How is what you are consuming and experiencing, and thus internalizing, *helping* you? Each singular moment, each singular choice, can be an opportunity for deepening more into your self and your purpose. What are you considering and questioning to get there?

Because questioning everything is one of my special skills, I'm sharing here a list of questions that I think about often. Some of these questions might sound like questions you've heard before or asked others, or they might even sound like your own questions. Very few questions, and very few concepts, are actually new. But I encourage you to look at these questions with a new lens.

Take several minutes to thoroughly think about each question. I also find it helpful to journal, sketch, or paint my answers to questions that I have difficulty thinking through or questions that keep resurfacing for me to consider. This is a good place to start on your questioning journey.

FOR THE RELATIONSHIPS AND CIRCUMSTANCES I WANT IN MY LIFE:

- What relationships am I currently in that I am tolerating?

- What relationships am I currently in that I am excited about?

- What relationships do I feel excited about putting my energy in moving forward?

- What are some characteristics of the type of people I want to spend my life around?

- What circumstances and relationships do I feel I've outgrown? Why am I still holding onto those? What's the difference between something feeling good because it is comforting and familiar, versus something feeling good because it is growing me?

- Who in my life am I trying to fix?

- Who in my life am I trying to heal?

- Where and with whom am I placing a lot of energy? Does the relationship feel reciprocal? If not, why am I still placing energy there?

- What parts of me are yearning to be accepted?

- What parts of me do I not accept? Why?

- When I am in an argument with a loved one, am I making anything more dramatic than it needs to be?

- How do I want to be treated by others?

- What am I impressed by? Is anything having to do with my own life on this list?

- What do I lie about to others? Why?

- What do I lie about to myself? Why?

- What feedback have people been trying to give me that I have been resistant to? Why?

- What am I practicing to enhance who I am? To enhance my health? To enhance my enjoyment of my life?

- How am I consciously designing the arc of my life?

FOR MY CAREER OR LIFE'S WORK:

- If I make a Venn diagram with the left circle headed "work that I need to do to pay the bills" and the right circle headed "work that I enjoy doing that excites me" (the middle overlap being work that fits both of these categories), then where on this list does most of my work fall?

- In Sebene Selassie's January 2022 newsletter, she shares that "vocation" originally comes from the Latin *vocare*, meaning "to call." "Vocation" was first used to refer to a spiritual calling and is inherently about listening. Am I actively listening to what moves and inspires me?

- Did I discard any part of me for the sake of security (financial or otherwise)? Can I begin to incorporate those parts again now?

TO CHECK (IN ON) MYSELF:

- What is my most toxic trait, and where and when have I noticed that I use it the most?

- What am I resistant to allowing myself to become? Why?

- What triggers my jealousy (for example: when I feel excluded, powerless, if I feel as though I am disappointing someone, disconnected, controlled, lonely, ignored)?

- What triggers my most toxic trait?

- What does my negative self-talk look like? How often do I notice it?

- Who am I most critical with? What traits do they have that I am critical of within myself?

- What have I not forgiven myself for? How would my life change if I did? Why do I feel I need to withhold my forgiveness of myself? Why do I feel I need to punish myself?

- What do I try hard to not think about? Why?

- Why do I compare myself to other people who are living a completely different life than I am and are on an entirely separate journey?

- What am I struggling with right now? Is there something small I can do today that will help—even if just for a moment?

- How often do I feel grateful?

- How often am I "just trying to get through" my life, rather than actually enjoying it?

- What deep wounds or feelings of being misunderstood am I holding onto?

- Whose behavior am I internalizing or making personal to me, instead of seeing it as a reflection of that person's inner emotional world?

- What am I avoiding?

- What do I do to numb in order to avoid? (Some common ways of numbing are eating, drinking alcohol, smoking weed, doing drugs, watching TV, and shopping online.)

- When I am experiencing a moment of pleasure, am I present with it? Do I elongate it or rush through it? Do I savor my pleasure?

FOUR

Let Yourself Be Visible

> My favorite images are the ones where
> Someone who isn't supposed to be there
> Who's like in a space, a space where
> We were not ever welcomed in, where we were not invited
> Yet we walk in and we show all the way up
> People try to put us down by saying
> "She's doing the most," or "He's way too much."
> But, like, why would we want to do the least?
>
> —JANET MOCK'S INTRODUCTION TO "JEWELRY"
> BY BLOOD ORANGE (TRACK 5 ON *NEGRO SWAN*)

I'VE BEEN THINKING ABOUT WHAT RUTH'S MOTHER, BO, SAYS IN THE 2018 sci-fi film *Fast Color*. For the entire movie, the family of Black women (Bo; Ruth; and Ruth's daughter, Lila) have to either stay in hiding or continue changing locations in order to conceal the supernatural powers (shifting tectonic plates, disintegrating solid matter, and controlling the Earth's elements) that they have inherited through their matriarchal lineage. For each of us, our superpower could be our ability to remain calm in the midst of conflict, our knowledge of how to connect with folks in a way that makes them feel seen, or our capacity to intuit what plants need just by looking at them. When Julia Hart wrote the movie, she said that she was inspired by her childbirth and that our ultimate power (especially as Black women) is creation.

When the family is finally captured, and Bo decides to free Ruth and Lila in exchange for her compliance in providing information to the white scientists (and I added "white" there because I think it's important to note that the scientists who want to capture and study these three Black women, like many other "doctors" and "scientists" over the past several hundred years, are white), she says: "We've stayed hidden because every time we came into the light, someone tried to take us, to hurt us. But that time is over now. You're scared because the world is dying and you don't know how to stop it, but I do. A new world is coming. This is only the beginning."

She gives this speech in front of a large group of white men who are actively threatening her. Her threat of being hurt is not necessarily removed with this visibility. But she knows that her strength comes in making herself visible, and with this visibility comes the embracing of her fullest self, the faith in her strength and all that she is capable of. When she says goodbye to her daughter and granddaughter, she says, "Don't worry, they can't hurt me now," implying that staying hidden has been the greatest pain and disservice to herself; by coming out of hiding, she has effectively emancipated her being, which is more powerful than anything that they might possibly try to do to her now that she has agreed to remain their captive. In this moment, she also embraces and affirms just how much power she actually knows herself to have. Bo shows us how powerful it can be to claim your visibility and stand confidently in your own strength and superpowers, especially in the midst of oppression.

SAFETY

But how can we be visible in a world where we don't feel safe? Safety is not always something that feels accessible to many of us. It is never your responsibility to feel safe, especially in a world that has systems that have literally been set up to destroy you. And you do not have to feel guilty for not opening up or being visible in times that you haven't felt safe. But how can we have agency in seeking out safe places for ourselves, and in making our body and mind, *ourselves*, a place where we can feel at home? And when you are able to find or create safe spaces for yourself, how can you choose to share yourself and bloom even more within these containers?

Often I feel like I'm a stranger to the world, not to the Earth, our most hospitable host, but to the world as it's been set up by other humans. I know logically that I am welcome to access and shop in stores, to use public transportation, to walk freely on the streets—but it's all so loud, so sharp, so filled with small talk and watching and desire and judgment. How could it actually be made for me? When I find a soft place to land, I savor it (and save it in my phone). It's so much work hosting, but oftentimes the spaces I create for others are the only ones in which I truly feel safe.

My mom once said that it made sense I was diagnosed with autism, because it explained a lot of the things I had openly communicated that I had dealt with in more recent years; but that when I was growing up, I was mostly quiet and never shared anything, so they "never knew anything was wrong." I never shared anything with them because despite my parents doing a great job at providing a safe container away from the outside world, I didn't always feel safe with them inside of it. As a child, I prided myself on not having anything wrong with me, since it seemed to me that my mom and dad already had a lot to deal with as young parents. And when things were wrong or I was upset, as in many Black households, I was critiqued for being "too sensitive" or "talking back disrespectfully" when sharing my feelings, or was threatened with a beating for crying too much or having a meltdown in public. I very quickly internalized the lessons they taught me for fear of physical violence: that I should be "seen and not heard," that I could be disciplined for small mistakes, and that not being "in control" of myself and my external emotional displays was completely unacceptable and, thus, a punishable offense. How could I be vocal about something and express how I feel when I'd never felt there was space for me to share my depth of feeling, to make a mistake, to have a meltdown? How can we be vocal when many of us, especially as Black women and femmes, are affirmed for "being strong," being respectable and palatable, and always having things pulled together? When we're actively policed (by society and our families) and taught our whole life that the "good girl" gets the prize, we begin to incorrectly internalize our needs as a burden to others. But I am allowed to have needs. As different humans learning ourselves and each other and doing our best in this ever-changing world, *we all are allowed to have needs.*

Looking back, I now see that I was a very troubled young person, always hiding. By the time I got to high school, I was so good at acting and masking, but was in such a troubled mental health space, that I secretly fantasized about jumping out of high windows and was frequently self-harming. Not even my closest friends knew the extent to which I was mentally suffering, because it was easier for me to let their problems take up the conversational space in our relationships. Even through my twenties, it was rare that I would actually share something I was struggling with. And when I did, my sharing was calculated and manipulative; I would disclose a piece of information I could share for the purpose of having a friend feel closer to me (because I recognized that people wanted to feel "let in"), but never anything that I actually felt vulnerable about. When I shared my diagnosis with a friend I've had since grade school, she wondered out loud, "But what are your symptoms? I grew up with you, and you've never seemed autistic." In contrast, when I've shared my diagnosis with some of my more recently made friends, friends with whom I have had years of close relationship in work and community, friends I've cried with and deep dived with and committed to, they have cried (!) tears of happiness; released a big sigh; laughed a tender cackle of knowing; said, "This makes *so* much sense"; and expressed new gratitude for now having language to understand how to be in closer relationship with me. The more I am comfortable with having and sharing my needs, making mistakes, and creating safe spaces within and around myself (as containers to hold my relationships), the more I allow people to know me, to *see* me, to love me.

VULNERABILITY

Choosing visibility is hard because of its direct demand for vulnerability. As humans, we crave connection. We feel better standing in a long line if someone comes to stand in line after us, even if it doesn't mean that we are any closer to our destination. We inherently want to feel that we can be related to easily and can relate to others. Being visible—potentially ostracizing or embarrassing yourself and thus potentially separating yourself from others—feels risky, and because of that risk, it takes vulnerability to make the choice to extend yourself to others. It is my experience that people are largely responsive and adaptable when I'm honest, vulnerable, and communicative of my needs. Why tell lies to make yourself smaller to fit in better with others, to appease?

I found that once I took a risk in actually sharing myself, people worked to figure out ways to support and love me better. Remember: *the people who love you always want to learn ways to love you better.* So why not share that information? It is a lesson in vulnerability and openness, and everyone wins. And if the folks you surround yourself with don't seem receptive to receiving and supporting a version of you that is more aligned with your growth, then maybe you need friends who will meet you in your vulnerability and desire for real connection. When's the last time you allowed yourself to do something that made you feel vulnerable, by yourself or in front of others? Tapping into this delicate softness within yourself is one of the first steps in finding strength in your visibility.

CLARITY

Another benefit of letting yourself be visible is that when you are, you can more clearly see the truest nature of others as well. When I'm meeting new people, my facial and vocal affect has been described as "blank" and monotone. I used to work hard to change it in social situations so that I might be more likable. I've observed that many people seem to be uncomfortable with this "blankness," or the empty space my affect creates that might typically be filled with social performance. People tend to project their internal state (and often their insecurities) onto it to fill the space, to project meaning onto it. When I am allowing myself to be genuinely me, I can more clearly see what people's true experiences are of themselves. People who are secure with themselves and open to discomfort tend to welcome me with open arms. People who are insecure or uneasy with a lack of social decorum have often assumed I'm disinterested, or being cold and intentionally mean to them, that I'm "a bitch." Take notice of how people respond to you when you aren't performing likability for them.

IMPOSTOR SYNDROME

Impostor syndrome is a feeling that many of us are familiar with: we feel like a fraud, unworthy of our current accomplishments or the space we're in. For my entire life until my autism diagnosis, I felt like an alien, someone not from this planet, in a vessel that was disguised as human. In social situations or when I was presenting my work or leading a workshop, I was nervous that I would perform in an "incorrect way," my very controlled mask accidentally slipping off for a moment, exposing the fact that I wasn't actually a "normal person," that I wasn't the human I claimed I was and the human they had hired or agreed to hang out with. People say you need to "fake it until you make it" as a remedy for internalized impostor syndrome. And I've spent much of my life masking in order to do just that, putting in the effort to fake what I perceive as a normal human experience, rather than just being comfortable with the one I am having.

I think that we should question why we have impostor syndrome in the first place. For nonwhite, disabled, non-straight-size, queer, and trans folks, the likely reason is that we've been taught to place value and importance on lives that do not look like ours. I recently got a tattoo with my friend Lee that says "human," to signify my acceptance of my inherent worthiness and value in the way that I am having and sharing my lived experience. Tattoos are a form of liberatory visibility work through the act of marking. We are making visible to the world who we really are, configuring our outsides to match our insides for that moment, until our bodies tell the time-stamped story of our lives to those around us. In *The Black Unicorn*, Audre Lorde writes, "I have been woman / for a long time / beware my smile / I am treacherous with old magic / and the noon's new fury / with all your wide futures / promised / I am / woman / and not white." There is strength in this claiming of our lives as nameable, valuable, and worthy. So what if we stop faking it?

I once went on a date with someone and they shared that they often fake their orgasms, which was a huge red flag for me. Even though, from an outsider's perspective, they seem to be a very publicly visible person, the most crucial part of self-visibility is giving yourself permission to experience life how *you* (and only you) can experience it, and knowing that your experience is "good enough" just as it is. You don't need to alter the expression of your experience to please someone else or make your life more palatable. It's not someone else's life. As motivational speaker Gary Vaynerchuk once said, "Other people might have a problem with the way you're living your life, but they're just sitting on the sidelines." Know that *you are valuable*, and your lived and true life experience is valuable enough that you can ground in it, you can advocate for it, you can share it.

RECLAIMING AGENCY AND VISIBILITY

Moving through my life as a multiracial, autistic, femme woman means that the world is told that it has access to all of me, all of the time—access to my smile and my interest when I'm walking down the street to get home, access to my labor when large brands ask me to "collaborate" with them for free in exchange for "promotion," access to my cultural traditions when white people decide to wear Native ceremonial headpieces for Halloween, access to my mental energy and expectations of my patience when I'm expected to "be less sensitive" when a restaurant is blasting music and has just turned on strobing neon lights above the bar. But I am able to reclaim agency over my body in my visibility, especially through practices such as BDSM.

BDSM helped me more clearly realize *who I am*. In BDSM, I can consensually choose to use my body for submission or service. I name myself as "kinky" and as a "leatherdyke" as a means of visibilizing myself and honoring the history of my ancestors and elders in these communities who came before me, and who oftentimes themselves did not feel safe being visible. As a femme-identified person, I am told that my "beauty" is of the highest value and importance, so I am able to reclaim for myself the power in that through "dollification," using my looks for play and fantasy. Fariha Róisín, in her most recent book *Who is Wellness For?*, says, "I think part of unlearning these vast and failing systems is to learn to trust ourselves and our own wisdom, but we must also challenge the status quo and unpack how we play into domination." It's important to remind ourselves that we have the power to decide what we do or don't do with our bodies always, and can determine when we want to engage with the structures that society has deemed useful or valuable (like in fantasy make-believe scenes), and when we want to fuck around with them, queer them, and ultimately dismantle them and anything else that doesn't serve us. And the first step in doing that is the claiming and the naming of ourselves, for ourselves.

In 2020, I was interviewed for a feature article for *Playboy* in which I talked about what it means to be Black and in the BDSM community. In it, we discussed that often, after playing, visible marks might be left on my body:

Elise's visible scarring is something she finds beautiful and a marker of both her Black and Indigenous heritage where scarification in certain communities is symbolic of a life lived, traumas survived and earned positions in society. "I find I am often expected to act 'lady-like,' meek, and shy. But having scars makes me feel strong. It's when I feel most like my outsides match with what my insides feel like."

My interviewing journalist, Tarisai Ngangura, agreed that "everything about living and breathing as a Black woman is politicized, making it an act of self-deception to believe that the bodies we are in do not determine the ways we perceive and are perceived by others, even in our most personal and sacred moments." The marks and scars are another act of living loudly in my truth. I go on to share that "being a Black woman in this world is definitely a very tough embodiment. One of the most beautiful things to me is looking at my Black body and seeing it in rope or seeing the marks that the rope, knives, or impact tools have made on my body. When I play, I feel like the fullest embodiment of myself."

SHAME

One reason that we resist visibility is shame. Similarly to the way self-internalized ableism affects autistic masking, many of us invisibilize ourselves, even subconsciously, because we feel shame about aspects of who we are. And it's not our fault! We've been bombarded with information our whole lives telling us that we are not good enough, not rich enough, not healthy enough, not straight enough, not white enough—so it makes sense that even the most radical of us have still internalized this messaging. Shame and vulnerability expert Brene Brown says, "We define shame as the intensely painful feeling or experience of believing that we are flawed and therefore unworthy of love and belonging—something we've experienced, done, or failed to do makes us unworthy of connection." Whenever shame arises on the surface, it's a signal that there might be something else happening several layers deeper.

One of the gifts of my autism is that I don't think I have ever actively experienced feelings of shame. I experience other feelings intensely, but not experiencing what folks describe to me as feelings of shame means that I haven't ever believed that I am unworthy of love and belonging because of something that I'm doing or experiencing. This gift helps me to clearly detect when people are experiencing shame and then give them the love and affirmation that they need, because what they're experiencing in that moment feels so clearly like disillusionment to me. Logically, we all need inclusion and affirmation and belonging, no matter what we've done (in other words, *fuck cancel culture*). So when shame comes up as a natural defense mechanism, could it be possible for us instead to get into practice of shifting feelings of shame toward ones of self-compassion? I love what author and illustrator Yumi Sakugawa says:

> *Shame is a self protective learned behavior that gives you conditional safety. You are safe if you hide, play small, blend in, please others, stay silent according to the expectations of others. You learn to self-shrink and dim your own lights to steer clear of conflict and pain. But self love is a self protective, learned behavior that gives you unconditional safety. No matter what others may think of you, you give yourself the space to be seen, follow your desires, and speak your truth. This is expansive safety where you are protected by your own radiance and self-acceptance.*

You are trusting yourself to be able to *count on yourself*, and in that act of trust, you are telling yourself *you are enough* and allowed to be present, public, and fully you!

We do not have to do anything more to be worthy; we are worthy just because *we are*.

I am Black & Indigenous, queer, autistic, a leatherdyke, femme, an energy worker and mystic, a womanist, and probably many more names and signifiers that I've yet to discover. When I talk with some folks in older generations, they've expressed frustration about millennials needing to have so many identifiers. And now Gen Zers seem to be even more into labeling themselves! Some elders ask, "If we're trying to get away from discrimination, then why do we all need to focus so much on our differences?" But the act of naming is both a conclusion as well as a beginning. It implies a process that first starts with encountering—a learning of self and a writing of your narrative. We are in survival mode when the recipe of our life is of someone else's choosing. But visibility helps us more clearly define who we *aren't*, so that we tell the story to others (and to ourselves) about who we *are*. Visibilizing and naming our differences for and with one another can help us to celebrate them, and ultimately our whole and full selves, more honestly.

So, I must ask: Who are you in the recipe of your life? And who do you want to become?

SELF-PORTRAIT
by Tatyana Fazlalizadeh

Self-portraiture is a record of my own existence. When I paint myself, I am making space for me to thoroughly look at myself—physically, emotionally, spiritually. Within that space, I am able to create an image that represents how I want to be seen and understood: powerful, vulnerable, bold, present. This is intentional for me as a person whose external identities have informed how others treat me. Transposing the white/male gaze, I'm creating my own gaze and meeting the viewer on my own terms.

Self Portrait (oil and acrylic on canvas; 48" x 72"; 2022)
Tatyana Fazlalizadeh

TATYANA FAZLALIZADEH (she/her) is a multimedia artist and author based in Brooklyn, New York. She creates portraits by way of community engagement and the public sphere, making site-specific work that considers how women and Black people experience race and gender. Her work has been presented in galleries, museums, and public sites across the globe. You can see more at @tylnnfaz.

FIVE

Get Used to Feeling Good

I was having a bumpy ride. I could sit there all day every day with my blabbering, deluded mind going on and on. But the only real possibility for creative response and for transformation was to invite kindness, get curious, cultivate ease, and smooth my own ride.

—SEBENE SELASSIE, *YOU BELONG: A CALL FOR CONNECTION*

I ONCE READ THAT THERE ARE ONLY TWO WAYS TO EXPERIENCE YOUR life: in a state of embodied presence or in a state of mental presence. Embodied presence is not as sensitive to your ever-changing stimulatory environment, whereas mental presence is. Working to get to a more consistent state of feeling good, which is actually just being in a state of embodied presence and physical awareness, is one of my continual life goals. When I allow myself to feel and experience even things that make me uncomfortable, rather than dissociating to avoid the discomfort (which actually prolongs the suffering even more), I experience a deeper sense of satisfaction in my life in general.

But it's pretty easy to live our lives through mental presence alone, and it's pretty easy to feel bad or dissatisfied. Especially if you have anxiety, depression, or other mental health struggles. Especially if you're a Black and/or Indigenous person, or another person of color, and you're queer, or nonbinary, or a woman or femme or trans or part of any other marginalized group that experiences the direct and indirect effects of structural and toxic oppression on a daily basis. Especially if your living, work, partnership, or family situation isn't the best. Especially if you don't have the living, work, partnership, or family structure that you're desiring. Especially if you are autistic and one of the symptoms of your autism is obsessive and compulsive looping thoughts and overprocessing. Especially if you're just a sensitive human in this world with daily stress living during a global pandemic, international war, and the threat of climate destruction. When we feel unwell because of our external circumstances, we learn early on that it starts to become safer to leave our bodies, leave our presence, and try to control, rationalize, and experience everything logically. But our overthinking is often causing us more suffering. Our not allowing the difficult feelings to be felt, and then pass, actually prolongs our affliction. What if being awake in our bodies—mindful of our presence and in tune with our senses and feelings as they ebb and flow in our current environment—and expressing our embodiment are actually among our most important resources, which can assist us in living with the most ease?

The Nondual Embodiment Thematic Inventory (NETI) is a twenty-item questionnaire that was developed by John Astin, David A. Butlein, and a team of experts to assess a heightened state of consciousness and awareness and to attempt to differentiate between people who have these ideas and those who actually live out their ideas at the deepest levels. The qualities that the scale assesses include compassion, resilience, propensity to surrender, interest in truth, defensiveness, capacity to tolerate cognitive dissonance and emotional discomfort, gratitude, frequency of nondual experience, anxiety level, motivational paradigm, authenticity, level of disidentification from the mind, and humility.

Let's take a moment to self-assess. Think about how often the following occur for you (some of these questions come directly from the NETI questionnaire):

- An inner contentment that is not dependent on objects or the actions of other people

- Accepting (not struggling with) whatever experience I am currently having (note: accepting the present does not mean that you shouldn't try to change it in the future if it isn't currently working for you)

- Feeling deeply at ease, wherever I am or whatever situation or circumstance I find myself in (and ease doesn't necessarily mean "easy." I can expect ease and flow while also expecting to work hard and that things might take more time than I expect)

- A sense of curiosity, openness to the possibility of my moment-to-moment experience

- A feeling of profound aliveness or vitality

- Feelings of gratitude or open curiosity about experiences

And finally, in what percentage of your life do you encounter "feeling good" or being in a stable sense of personal satisfaction?

Let's break this down. First, I don't like attributing positive or negative associations to my feelings. In other words, I don't think that feelings should be judged on a binary scale of negative or "bad" feelings versus positive or "good" feelings. Instead, I use "feeling good" as a colloquial and inclusive phrase that can have a wide variety of meanings. If you ask someone how they're doing and they say "good," that response doesn't minimize the complexity of their life experience but, to me, means that in that moment, they are firmly here. In that moment, they are present to our connection and, in that, they feel good.

To me, "feeling good" doesn't just mean feeling "happy," and I believe that people whose brains chemically don't have access to happy feelings most of the time can still access a general sense of "feeling good." For this reason, I also like to think of "feeling good" as a means of describing a sense of personal satisfaction. Even when you are struggling with tough feelings, it's still possible to experience an overarching sense of personal satisfaction. I also think that people like me, who have nonstop, overactive, compulsive thinking as a symptom of an atypical mental experience, can also "feel good." "Feeling good," to me, more simply means that I'm perceiving feeling present in my whole being (not just logically or in my mind) and rooted in my body. When I am in this state of "feeling good," all my (sometimes very complex and tangled) feelings exist at the same time, without my attributing a positive or negative marker to them, which I think is actually one of the keys to "feeling good": I'm allowing my feelings and thoughts to come and go, passing through like temporary visitors, so that the underlying way I feel is peaceful and mindful of my presence. I feel whole and principled within myself. I like thinking about my "feeling good" as being in a state (regardless of which temporary emotional or thought visitors are also present) of timeless, or time-suspended, observation. Because of my embodied presence, I am in a heightened state of awareness to observe or to pay attention, and I am thus open to experiencing a deepened sense of gratitude and personal satisfaction.

Spiritual teacher and speaker Tara Brach, in her talk on embodied presence, referred to philosopher Jiddu Krishnamurti's musings on love: "To pay attention means we care. Which really means we love." She goes on to share that "attention is the most basic form of love. So by learning to pay attention to our inner aliveness, becoming embodied into the living world, we fall in love with our world" and, I would also argue, with ourselves.

Some of my most recent moments of "feeling good," or moments of rooted embodiment and paying attention to my inner aliveness, looked like responding to conflict in a calm way, despite the high stress of an argument; having a conversation with a friend and really listening to what they had to say; experiencing my senses activated in a grounding way (not in an overstimulated way) during a BDSM scene; and feeling energetic and vivacious in my body after a tough workout. I encounter these states of being when I host friends in my home and someone gives an audible sigh of pleasure, and I can tell they've let go of themselves a little bit more than they have in a while; when I take the first sip of a wine so deeply amber-hued when it comes out of the bottle, sunlight bouncing around the glass, that it makes me gasp; when my lover asks me if I'm okay after the intensity of our connective energy exchange; when I share a boundary with a friend, and they say, "I hear you," and respect it; when my body is suspended in rope, and the pain is overwhelming my senses so that I cannot think or overthink about anything other than that moment; when I'm watering my plants, fingering the veins of the leaves, marveling in wonder at their new growth; when I'm walking down my block, admiring the trees changing colors and the way they do this so effortlessly, so knowingly and assuredly; the moment after

I tell the truth, even if it initially felt difficult to share; when I'm feeling the breeze lightly sweeping past my shoulders on the evening of what was a humid summer day in the city, evaporating the sticky sweat on the back of my neck that's been gathering there in the sunshine; when I'm sweaty and dirty on a hike, and I can smell the moisture in the living air pulsing all around and within me; when I take time to put on music before cooking, knowing I'm about to treat myself to the slowness of the moment. These singular moments of embodiment, which aren't always possible to access (even when I'm in similar circumstances), feel like satisfying completions of the circles in my self / my cells. In my "feeling good" states, I feel gratifyingly complete. My mind is without excessive thinking for that moment, and I am mindful and in flow with the environment around me. My focus is open, and I am paying attention to feeling deeply present in my body.

Some of these feelings may not be accessible to you the majority of the time, or ever. I have friends with chronic pain who simply don't have access to feeling physically well in their bodies. This doesn't mean that there aren't a variety of other ways that they can access their version of "feeling good." And the environments in which you "feel good" are fully customizable (spoiler alert: just like most other things in your life!) and are also always changing. When you're fifteen, feeling good might look completely different to you from the way it looks when you're in your forties—or it might look the same. The point is for you to think of different times that you "feel good," times of embodied presence, and ways that you can access that core feeling of present mindfulness and embodiment more often.

Once you've defined a few times when your state of "feeling good" has revealed itself to you, I want you to think about these questions: What percentage of your life right now is spent experiencing that? And what percentage is spent outside of this state of being?

And now, let's ask ourselves: Why is our "feeling good" percentage lower than 90–100 percent? Unless you're in a temporary external circumstance that will soon pass and that you have no control over (and my next question would be why you feel you don't have control or agency to change something in your life that doesn't leave you "feeling good"), then why isn't more of your current life spent "feeling good"?

With most of us, it usually isn't a temporary external circumstance that has us living outside of our "feeling good" moments more frequently than not; it's actually more about our internal state. Once we *give ourselves permission* to access a changed and elevated internal state more regularly, we can actively and intentionally structure our lives in a way that allows for us to have both inner and external peace more often as well. And giving myself permission for my embodied presence also helps me to get over myself—my overthinking and my striving to become a better version of myself for my self, get over my ideas that constitute my ego Self, and move past my stories that separate my Self from all other living things.

I was once one of those people who thought that I could feel good only a certain portion of my life and that the rest of my life had to be spent working, in struggle, fighting with friends and partners, and so on. I subconsciously created turmoil around me, mirroring the chaos I felt internally in my mind. I didn't know this consciously, of course; I was just acting on instincts of discomfort. But once I committed to "feeling good" as a practice, I saw just how much time I had spent giving myself permission to not feel the best and how much energy I had allocated subconsciously to bringing myself down from "feeling good" states so that I could be back in my comfort zone of feeling okay. I watched myself existing in cycles—working hard to be in these states of presence, peacefulness, and ease and then once I arrived, immediately self-sabotaging and ending up back where I started. Whether it was with external systems that I had set up for myself (such as an 8 a.m.–6 p.m., five-days-a-week job that I didn't enjoy) or with internal systems of self-destruction (such as frequently drinking way past my limit so that I could "relax," even though I knew the alcohol would destroy my body and mental health for the next couple of days), I was making decisions in a self-detrimental cycle. I was doing so because without realizing it, I had subconsciously given myself permission to "feel good" for a little more than half of the time (let's say 60 percent of the time), while 10 percent of the time I spent crashing into the depths of my mess, and the other 30 percent I spent struggling to get back to that "feeling good" place. Somewhere along my journey, I had apparently subconsciously decided that I would feel good only in specific situations: when I wasn't working on the weekends, when I was on vacation, when I was on a date—times when I had specifically given myself permission to release my shoulders, have a glass of wine, take a deep breath, and enjoy myself.

Why do we do this to ourselves? Why do we live in cycles of self-punishment or self-loathing? Why do we, again, let other people and larger cultural narratives command our feelings and emotions? Why is "feeling good" for certain people only, but never ourselves? Why is "feeling good" for monetizable moments only, such as when we are spending money on a trip or paying for services at a spa? Why is "feeling good" allowed only when we are in spaces that the culture has communicated to us are "feel good" spaces?

We must remember: there are no designated spaces. There are no requirements.

I didn't consciously realize that I could actually access "feeling good" for most of my life, even when I was working (gasp). I could access a present mindfulness and embodiment as an internal state and approach each activity with a perspective of ease. For example, right now as I'm working on this chapter, I'm sitting by a rooftop pool in Chicago looking out at a dramatic view of the city, surrounded by plants and lush green, drinking a delicious and energizing tea, and considering putting my bathing suit on soon. This doesn't mean that my obsessive and looping thoughts are gone; being autistic is my life experience and will *always* be my life experience. But I'm finally in a place (most of the time!) where I'm not as worried about trying to control those thoughts.

In the December 16, 2022, episode of *The One You Feed* podcast, the host Eric Zimmer shares: "There's an event, and then there is my view of that event, and in between those two things I create and assign a meaning. . . . But recognizing that process and asking the question 'what am I making this mean and what else can it mean?' is a profoundly liberating question." What if we are able to mindfully observe, and change, the meaning that we're attaching to our circumstances? With each moment, you can make the choice to choose curiosity, to create space around your approach to that particular moment. And if there are many moments in your life when you feel that your situational external experience leaves you feeling not the best (that is, you're having an experience that you would not choose again), and you're finding it challenging to access this mindful presence within yourself, the next questions to think about are these: Why are you in this experience to begin with? What's holding you back from creating a life in which you have more agency in the future? What's stopping you from having more of a say over how your time is spent? Why can't you have more access to spaciousness? Why shouldn't you have the opportunity to access your life experiences from a perspective of ease and flow and expansion, instead of anxiety and close-mindedness and contraction?

ALLOWING GOOD FEELINGS

So why does it seem as though so many of us have a subconscious block around feeling good—as if feeling good is something to feel guilt or shame around? Why does it seem that it's an elusive goal that we aim for but never actually achieve (similar to "rest"; see Chapter 1: "Fuck Being Busy")—or that we achieve it, but never in a sustainable and long-lasting way? And why do we feel attached to the percentage of time we spend "feeling good" in our present lives that we've already subconsciously determined and currently live by (see Chapter 3: "Question Everything")? What if we can allow ourselves to "feel good" for more time? Instead of letting our subconscious story dictate how we experience our lives, what if we can consciously choose to create more space to access our "feeling good" states more often? And for those of us who aren't neurotypical, what if we can acknowledge and appreciate the individual obstacles (and superpowers) of our minds and our bodies as truth, but not let that be the end or most defining factor of our story? Why are many of us choosing to live in a very limited state of feeling okay, when there's the possibility to live within the expanded awareness of feeling great; achieving ever-growing creativity, fulfillment, and abundance; and accessing a greater state of awareness with each new day?

I began thinking about all of these things when I read Gay Hendricks's *The Big Leap* several years ago, and (I'm not saying this lightly) it changed my life. In the book, he shares the term "upper limiting," and learning about that concept has greatly influenced how I manage the tone of my thoughts and consider the level of agency I have in my life. An "upper limit" is a self-imposed barrier, or limit, *that we put on ourselves*—whether it's a barrier on our level of success, our "feeling good," our relationship happiness, our job satisfaction, or how well our life is going in general. Of course, we are working within the realms of what our current mind and body offer us; we don't have to dismiss the times where we don't feel the best, either. But Hendricks argues that if we consciously choose to increase the amount of time each day that we feel good, allowing things to go well in our life most or even all of the time, we can live in greater harmony, intimacy, and prosperity. And I don't know about you, but I am here for this!

Once I began noticing my upper-limit problems (all the ways I was subconsciously getting in my own way), I saw how much energy I was wasting on justifying the limitations in my life, instead of choosing to cultivate a mindset of possibility and expansion— being open to the premise that it's possible to "feel good," access embodied presence and awareness frequently, and have my life go well for more time than I had even considered before.

These are small and large ways I have caught myself upper limiting:

- I've intellectualized my feelings of joy and excitement, because it feels safer than letting myself feel what it's like to have everything I've ever wanted—that I am finally existing in a personal reality where I am receiving a lot of what I've manifested and worked hard for.

- I've started a fight with a lover after a great day together in order to subconsciously create space and separation, instead of just saying out loud, "I would like some time by myself now."

- Resting on my couch feeling relaxed and positive, I've suddenly, seemingly out of nowhere, started to panic about the state of the world and begun to feel guilty that I'm lucky enough to have my own couch to rest on and my own apartment to live in. Then I've quickly gotten up and started cleaning or doing work, feeling "too guilty" and anxious to relax.

- I've not asked for the money that I know I deserve when discussing a quote with a catering client or for a brand influencer campaign, because I don't want them to say no.

- I've felt so nervously excited for an upcoming date or work gig that I've gone out the night before and partied too hard, thus sabotaging my ability to be at my best for the event that I had been looking forward to.

Hendricks asks us to ask ourselves, "Am I willing to feel good and have my life go well all the time?" He then argues that "saying yes to that question is one of the most courageous actions a human being can take. In the face of so much evidence that life hurts and is fraught with adversity on all fronts, having a willingness to feel good and have life go well all the time is a genuinely radical act." As a Black & Indigenous, queer, autistic femme woman living in a society that often tells me (both directly and indirectly) that I'm valued mostly by my level of labor output in service of others and thus that my personal pleasure and happiness should not be prioritized as a focus in my life, choosing a life where I'm actively allowing myself to live without self-imposed limitations is an almost inconceivable and *incredibly* radical act.

We humans are made of the same materials as the natural world; we have ecosystems within us. Our bodies follow the rhythms and patterns in nature, filled with intuitive knowing, flowing, and sustaining (without thinking) that hold up these natural systems. Our human brains' overthinking is actually what destroys us. But if we instead listen to the quiet hum of what our system is saying as it tugs at us with "friendly reminders," how much different (easier) would our lives be? If we're feeling tired, why don't we rest? If we are thirsty, why don't we have some water? If we need to use the bathroom (regardless of how "inconvenient" we think it might be to those around us), why don't we use the bathroom? I can't tell you how much energy I've wasted thinking about how badly I have to pee and trying instead to force myself to focus on work, a show, falling asleep—when actually, as soon as I feel I have to use the bathroom, I can just go, be present in that relief, and then immediately get back to whatever else I was doing. Similarly, if someone offers you something that could help you, hydrate you, or relieve some stress—take the help! After my partner got top surgery, I wasn't allowed to stay overnight with them in the hospital (because COVID visiting hours suck). They offered to get me a car service home so that I didn't have to walk fifteen minutes back to the train in misting rain with my heavy bags—and I almost said no. But then I caught myself and gladly accepted the help/love. But why did I almost turn down the offer? Why would I choose "roughing it out" when I could just choose ease? If I chose to walk, my back would be hurting, the train ride would likely be overstimulating (because when is it not?), and I would arrive home with less capacity and energy for my own self-care after such a long day, and thus would have less to give my partner when I picked them up the next day; I would have less energy to do and be my best. We make up rules for what we think we should be doing instead of offering ourselves the nurturance our body systems tell us we need. This subconscious practice is an internalized reflection of our upper limiting and self-sabotage.

TOXIC POSITIVITY

Just as harmful as our internalized upper limiting, but masquerading as a friend, is our culture's "toxic positivity." Toxic positivity is the pressure (either external pressure, or internal pressure that we put on ourselves) that we should have a positive mindset in response to emotional pain or a difficult experience. Negative emotions are seen as inherently bad, and positivity and happiness are irrationally pushed. Because of this toxic positivity, we end up judging ourselves for our sadness, blah-ness, jealousy, anger, insecurity, and so on—all feelings that are part of a healthy and ever-changing human experience—instead of just allowing ourselves to experience them. Judging typically leads to minimizing and invalidating ourselves, instead of just allowing the intense or tough feelings to flow out naturally.

Author and researcher Katherine May, in her book *Wintering: The Power of Rest and Retreat in Difficult Times*, writes, "Sometimes the best response to our howls of anguish is the honest one. We need friends who wince along with our pain, who tolerate our gloom, and who allow us to be weak for a while, while we're finding our feet again." We all need to get more comfortable with allowing our friends, and ourselves, to have feelings and experiences that aren't all positive. In a conversation with Krista Tippett on the *On Being* podcast, May said:

> *I think we're so uncomfortable with sadness. And our instinct, when someone tells us they're sad, is to solve it for them or to find a message that's going to inspire them. And I think that can feel a lot like being pushed away . . . . It's a skill that we can all learn to . . . open up a space that their sadness is acknowledged*

and validated .... And I think we're often afraid of opening the door to it, because we see it as this unruly thing. But my belief is that it's only unruly when it's being pushed away and when we're only ever allowed to glance it from the corner of our vision; that actually, when you make a space for your sadness to come into, it's a known thing. It's something that we actually can understand and that we can be with and work with. It's not terrifying. What's terrifying is the flinch away from it.

This flinching away from it, or the act of toxic positivity, can look like any of these:

· Using positive justifications to delegitimize hardship or real experiences of anxiety, fear, and sadness

· Denying or minimizing your experience or feelings because other people have it harder than you

· Pretending to be happy, or "save face," to try to convince yourself or others that things are okay even when they aren't

· Judging your looping thoughts, intense feelings, or heavy emotions as "negative" or "weak" and not allowing yourself to experience them (through blocking them off, compartmentalization, disassociating, escapism, avoidance, and so on)

- Rewarding yourself for avoiding your more intense feelings (for example, telling yourself, "Phew! I'm so happy I didn't allow myself to cry at that moment. That would have been pathetic.")

- Telling yourself that you should feel *only* positive and grateful because you have a lot of great things going on in your life

- Your social media friends posting about all the positive things they're working on in a pandemic and encouraging others to change their perspective to "hustle" and "grind" to do the same, effectively encouraging a minimization of any valid feelings of uncertainty or sadness

- Intellectualizing your feelings with a positive spin, instead of allowing yourself to experience them as they feel

A 1997 psychological study about emotional regulation by J. J. Gross and R. W. Levenson concluded that suppressing or inhibiting our feelings often leads to increased psychological stress and problems such as insomnia or disrupted sleep, anxiety, acute stress, prolonged grief, risk of substance abuse, and even post-traumatic stress disorder.

As an autistic person, I don't often know the "correct" response when someone is sharing something with me. I've often gotten into further conflict with partners because I'll get frustrated that even after I've gone through the list of the things they've asked me to do during a conflict (apologize, take accountability, reach out to touch them, repeat back to them what they have said to me about their feelings), they don't feel connected, because to them I'm still visibly frustrated, annoyed, upset, or rushing them to move on. And then I'm confused, because I've done the things they want, but it's not what they needed in order for us to move forward. It's not that I don't feel empathy; I do, deeply (arguably, too much). But once I've quickly processed the difficult feelings, I am ready to move on, whereas my neurotypical partners take more time processing their feelings and need a bit more time to open up into their vulnerability to reestablish a connection point with me. It's important to allow for different methods of processing, responding, and communicating while establishing and nurturing your relationships with others, all while allowing time for yourself to first sit with, and then move through, feelings that might be uncomfortable.

MAKING SPACE FOR IT ALL

With the surge of social media "flawlessness" as a portrayal of our lives and the use of social media as a distraction from dealing with uncomfortable feelings, many of us have fallen into these patterns of "toxic positivity" or other unintentionally harmful ways of thinking. So here's a reminder (for me as well as for you):

- You are allowed to have days where you feel down, unwell, or even horrible! Our feelings and states of being, just like everything else, include a broad spectrum of experience in order to create for us a whole and full adventure. That doesn't make you any less grateful for the favorable things happening in your life.

- You are allowed and encouraged to feel and experience all of your intense feelings. They aren't too much, too messy, or too complicated.

- The way that your brain works is the way that it works—whether it's slow to process, hyperactive, or compulsive. Even if it feels painful and exhausting sometimes, there are also many times that it benefits you and takes care of you.

- You are allowed to erect boundaries around the type of "advice" you receive from your family and friends. If someone in your life is always telling you that you need to "be positive," and you don't feel that they make space for your wide spectrum of feelings, then you are allowed to create boundaries around when and how often you engage with them.

- You are allowed to have needs and ask for help. Having needs doesn't make you weak; in fact, knowing when you don't have the capacity and need assistance is a strength that should be celebrated.

- You are allowed to ask for affirmation and reassurance when you feel you need them.

- You are allowed to have intense feelings or emotions about something even when it seems that other people around you aren't as affected by the same experience.

- You (and your partners and friends) are allowed to take as much time as needed to process uncomfortable or painful feelings. But you must not allow these feelings to overstay.

"Feeling good" doesn't mean dismissing the bad feelings, the sticky and looping obsessive thoughts; it's about recognizing that our reality is often a reflection of our inner world. It's about choosing in each moment whether you will respond with haste or with fear—or whether you will respond (and receive) with curiosity and love. Practicing somatic embodiment helps resonate our thinking. It begins to shift our mental changes (things we've thought about and processed in our mind) into change we can experience at a body level—transforming the habitual historical patterns into new ways of being. "Feeling good" is about treating your feelings as passing and prioritizing adjusting your inner landscape to one that's forever open to abundance, open to observance. Author and artist Mimi Zhu shares that "I learn these lessons from the land, as I envision the ocean and its enduring moving waves, the trees and their falling leaves, and the sun as it rises and sets each day. Consider your emotions as an element of the earth: coming, being, and washing away."

NATURAL STATE
by Maya Harder-Montoya

I dreamed this end to the world: the summer before, four nights in a row, the race of infection and detection—graying faces, hollow eyes, and foreheads beaded in sweat; a warped blur of worldwide illness and dwindling food supplies. I was in a long field, then a series of half-torn-out cars, then awake and sobbing into my silver sheets. I haven't thought about these dreams much since, mostly because they represent one small fragment of the hundreds of apocalypses I have visited over the years—a drop in the bucket of alternative realities.

What I have thought about, almost every day, for many days, is Cassandra. Appropriate, considering our current mass-level extinction event, to find prayers for the patron saint of the mad and the gaslit. In some versions of the story, Apollo delivers her curse by spitting into her mouth, which is too perfect a metaphor for every terrible ex-partner we all had when we were grasping our way through our twenties. When I imagine her, she is tending to the plants that surround the temple, pausing to stroke leaves that curl toward white stone steps, grateful for the softness of their touch. She is steadfastly genuine in her attempts to warn the world of its destructive failings, but not prophesize after the fact—most likely because the world is really interested only in its own destruction. The world and I have that much in common.

I used to feel like a memory that changed with every retelling, fragmented and regarded only in relation to something outside myself. I used to think that this was a natural procedure, everything defined by its outer limits, but over time it became clear that this grain of an idea was preventing me from accessing a space of true self-reflection.

When I finally got my diagnoses, it felt like being handed a sheet of paper: a pink slip, releasing me from any imagined future of stability. I did what so many of us rightly do—as gently as possible, I bent and folded the reality of my night terrors, my suicidal ideations, my many days called in "sick" to school or work, into a beautiful talisman. A paper crane built to protect me from shame. A lovable creature I could hold with the care that I so desperately wanted, and rarely received, from the people around me.

For a long time, it was just me and my paper crane. Like some endangered cranes who are raised in captivity, I was also unsure if I belonged to the species I was labeled. A failure of nature. In my dreams, I pass smoothly from one reality to the next, thin veils that brush aside as easily as reeds along the water's edge. Why would I choose to stay in this particular colonial nightmare when I could easily slip into the next life, leaving my body to the nearest river?

It would be an oversimplification to say that entheogenic medicine saved my life. A more accurate understanding is that Indigenous medicinal practice involves an active and loving partnership with the living planet. When I began investing in some of these practices, tending to my spindling roots, I began to consider myself a being within that partnership; my relationship to the land became a literal mirroring of my relationship to myself. If the Earth was living, then perhaps I was, too.

Plants are ungovernable, and they have the aggressive curiosity of children: whatever versions of freedom the world presents us, they know a mockery when they see one. What I was ultimately desirous of wasn't happiness or healing, but liberated growth. Seeding as riot. Voracious bloom. What would good feel like, when released from the colonial expectation of a "natural state"? According to whose nature, and what interests?

Of course, there is a grand cognitive dissonance that is practiced daily to accept any number of "natural states"—poverty, violence, subjection. The 2021 meme version puts this question even more succinctly: "Am I mentally ill, or just living through late-stage capitalism?" The machine of the industrial world runs on binaries, and therefore, we have been given only the binary of sickness and health to describe our sensory and spiritual experiences.

It took me so long to accept and find strength in my own mental illness; what would it be like to try and untangle the truth of a much more complicated and nuanced reality? A small flutter, a live beating heart in my paper crane, a wide dark eye fixed on my present body. As much as I am blood and bone, I am gray space. As solid as I sit upon the Earth, I am fluid, and more precious for it. I am sick, and I am not. My natural state is contradiction. There is so much joy to be found in contradiction.

When asked, I tend to describe the effects of medicinal psilocybin in terms of decibels: if my depression is a cacophony of detachment and exhaustion, microdosing turns the volume down to a background level. A minor-key composition that now follows me from room to room, but no longer drowns out my thoughts. There are chambers in my body now, for softer and more familiar songs.

My dreams are the same, still billowing and apocalyptic, but now I can shape-shift in the daytime too. Fungi medicine gives me permission to be a creature. My olfactory sense is always the first thing to greet the earth, caught on a slight breeze or a change in direction, and at once the depth of the soil is up and into my body. Dense and clean, rotting leaves and soft moss underneath me. I can smell the difference between one warm tree and its sibling. Hear a small round lizard move in winding steps through the underbrush. Taste the crisp difference in the air in the exact moment the sun drops below the horizon. As a creature, my body belongs to itself again, in this future, and all the others.

Fungi have their own gift of prophecy; they have built their own temples to generational wisdom. What a pleasure to see mycelium receive the worship it deserves, as a connector of vast and ancient knowledge, a monument of collective symbiosis. If we are moving parts of the same shifting organism, are the Cassandras among us simply placed at a higher vantage point than the others? The outermost layer of skin on the tips of outstretched fingers: the first to scorch, the first to freeze, the first to know.

An act of love is remembering that when I stand among plants, I am standing among kin. The care I was once desperate for is the gentleness of my own hands when I hold a smooth branch with three fingers, steadying myself as I move from one stone to another along the river. The days I feel most radiant in myself are the days that I am the river. A river is neither happy or unhappy; it's just moving—all separate parts as a whole, flashing in the sunlight, rushing to meet the rocks.

MAYA HARDER-MONTOYA (they/them) is a New Mexico–born writer, editor, and journalist based in Lenapehoking. Their work explores queerness as metaphysics, fetish as storytelling, and marginalized bodies as sites of ecological innovation. Their writing and interviews can be found in numerous publications including *Artforum*, *Posture*, *PAPER*, *The Archive* of the Leslie-Lohman Museum of Art, and zines such as *FIST*. They are currently working on a collection of poetic essays that may or may not be a novel. Follow them at @mayaceleste.

SIX

Choose Who You Want to Be

"Baby, [there is] a world where I can name myself anything . . . For so much of my life, I've been shrinking. When I was a kid, I thought I was big enough to have every right to name something out of this world, and then I just started shrinking myself. By the time I met you, I'd already gotten so small. And I thought you knew how big I wanted to be. I thought you saw me . . ."

"I see you now, Hippolyta Freeman, and I want you to be as big as you can be," he says.

"I am Hippolyta, Discoverer."

—HIPPOLYTA AND GEORGE FREEMAN,
LOVECRAFT COUNTRY (SEASON 1, EPISODE 7)

I WAS IN MY MIDTWENTIES WHEN I REALIZED THAT I COULD ESSEN-tially choose who I wanted to be in my life—that, as in a video game, I could essentially "pick my player." My birth chart, my ancestral lineage, my genetics, and my past actions were very significant, yes, but only a part of the story. Like many of us, I had been journeying on a socially constructed and suggested path for my entire life, but had suddenly discovered what seemed like a major life hack: I didn't have to do any of the things that had been suggested to me. And in fact, I could actually just do anything that I wanted to do. If what my family and society wanted seemed to be in alignment with what felt good for me, then great! But if not, I could actually just choose "me" every. single. time.

Since having this perspective shift, it's become glaringly obvious to me, through an intuitive tug that I've learned to pay close attention to, when I am not choosing something that feels best aligned for me. And it's also become very noticeably apparent when other people aren't choosing themselves or when they're placing more power on their social identity markers than is necessary. I hear comments like these all the time: "Even though I don't want to, I have to go to my parents' house for the holidays because I've been going every year." "My Venus is in Scorpio, so I am inherently sneaky in romantic relationships." "I grew up with a parent who was always deflective and avoidant, so I guess this is who I am, too." We see this modeled all the time in the media, too. Like any good dyke, when I watched Shane sabotage her wedding with Carmen on *The L Word* (the OG not the reboot), I was very upset. She saw her father cheating on his wife, and it sent her into a self-destructive spiral. For a moment, she believed that she could create the future she wanted for herself with Carmen, but when she confronted her father on his cheating, she concluded that it was inevitable that she would be unfaithful and sabotage the love in her life because it was in her genes. Major eye roll.

This thing of "following the rules of social expectations" and "following expectations that others have of me because of a predetermined life path" has always felt so silly to me. Yes, I understand that we have certain responsibilities to people we love in order to maintain and nurture our relationships with them, and, yes, I do feel inherently complicated (and sometimes sneaky), and I happen to have Venus in Gemini, so I notice myself getting bored in romantic relationships easily and want to be stimulated with the next exciting thing. And before I knew that I could create a life that responds to my nature and functioning systems that help me not to overindulge that nature (such as a polyamorous relationship structure, so that I don't have to feel guilty about having other interests, and a communication foundation with my partners that is honest and forthcoming, so that I feel intimately known), I was cheating on partners all of the time. I just felt that this was who I was, so there was no way to change it. But there are ways to acknowledge our nature, choose who we want to be, and then create systems of accountability that help us achieve those goals. There are also ways to identify what doesn't feel good in current relationships (even ones that we've had our whole lives), and create new boundaries so that we can feel better in them. We don't need to follow the social rules or succumb to our baser instincts.

One could argue that self-sabotage is inevitable. The second law of thermodynamics implies that, like everything, the body and mind will naturally deteriorate over time without intentional intervention. Everything naturally dissolves into chaos. But we can choose to intervene and restore order as much as possible. We can choose not to create a conflict in our relationships whenever they're feeling a little mundane. As we age, our life energy decreases (which explains why children often run circles around us, because they have so much more of it). But we can choose to increase our life energy by increasing the amount of excitement we feel in our lives, how much we laugh, the frequency with which we have sex and physical connection with others, how often we experience love, and more. Instead of self-sabotaging, we can get curious about what our underlying needs are. Do we need attention, rest, excitement? How do we choose to give ourselves what we need instead of self-sabotaging?

SPROUTING

Abraham Lincoln once said that people are just as happy as they make up their minds to be. I disagree with the simplicity of this statement, because I feel it minimizes the complexity of the mental health struggles that many of us deal with on a day-to-day basis. But I do like to think of the chemicals my brain was born with, the natural and inherent ways that I am, and my past circumstances all as the soil that my growth can spring from. So if we, as tender seeds,* are starting with some pretty shitty soil—soil that is not the most conducive for high growth conditions—we might need to get extra sunlight or a different watering system from the one that other seeds, situated in a more nutrient-dense soil, might need. We also might need to pack in some of the more nutrient-dense soil to mix into ours, so that we will be homed in better conditions. But with either soil option, we aren't doomed. We just need to be able to figure out what we require based on our current conditions and then use the resources around us to make our current conditions more suitable to what we need to sprout, to grow upward.

And this goes deeper than family holiday expectations or my relationships in my twenties: I watch people turn down job opportunities, new experiences, and travel to unfamiliar places because they don't fit with the current story of themselves that they have made up in their heads. Even if they want to change or see themselves in a different light, being outside of their comfort zone leads to impostor syndrome, which can then feel like negative reinforcement for trying on their new story. So they go back to the version that feels the safest.

---

* This metaphor is in direct reference to conversations with my close friend Tara Aura, and our past work with our co-created project Blind Seed.

And especially if you're queer, a femme, a woman, a person of color, have darker skin, are differently abled, fat, gender-nonconforming, or any identity outside of the "right" ones that have been drilled into our heads our whole lives, your experience of impostor syndrome is likely just how you're experiencing life under a patriarchal, misogynistic, able-bodied, fatphobic, capitalistic, white supremacist society (see Chapter 4: "Let Yourself Be Visible").

But I'm here with a little hint: you can actually change your life story whenever you want. You can't change the past—obviously—but you can move on from it. And the first step is to acknowledge your past (all the harm, the hurt, the trauma, the self-narratives, the projected narratives you've internalized). The second step is to take responsibility for having the agency to change your life and to believe that you actually can. And the third step is intentionally deciding to create a different future story of yourself.

In *Karma: A Yogi's Guide to Crafting Your Destiny*, Jaggi Vasudev says "it is important to see that whatever seems determined in your life has been determined by you unconsciously. You have written your own software." He goes on to explain:

> *Once that software is written, your whole system functions accordingly. Based on the information from the past, certain memory patterns keep recurring. Now your life turns habitual, repetitive, and cyclical. Over time, you become ensnared by*

your patterns. Like so many people, you probably don't know why certain situations keep recurring in your inner and outer life. This is because these patterns are unconscious. As time goes on, you turn into a puppet of your accumulated past . . . . However hard [you] try to emerge from it, [you] keep falling into a trap. If one does not consciously rewrite one's karmic software, the regularity of the pattern can feel like it is being imposed from without, rather than initiated from within. But this software is not a fate to be endured. It can be rewritten, dropped, or distanced.

In fact, people do this all the time when they are faced with a life-altering situation and are thrown outside of their comfort zone. How often do you read stories about someone surviving something traumatic (a plane crash, terminal cancer, a huge breakup, the death of a loved one), which then becomes the jumping-off point for shifting their entire life? After a major external catalyst, people often feel they've been given a second chance to do things "right," and they end up doing what they knew they should have been doing all along, such as coming out about a truth they had kept hidden, making amends with their friends or family, or cherishing someone special in their life more than they had before. But we don't need traumatic events to occur in order to change our lives. It's actually quite masochistic of us to sit around waiting for these really difficult and painful upheavals in order to catapult change, instead of just making the decision to change on our own—right now, today—for no other reason than to be more aligned with who you are and who you want to be. In reading this chapter so far, I bet you've already had the familiar pang of knowing, of resonance. You likely already know what you want to change. So what's holding you back? And why are you overcomplicating things?

NEUROPLASTICITY

Brain cells called neurons are essentially the building blocks of our brains, the information transmitters between us and the sensory world we live in. And our neural pathways, the connections that form between our neurons, give meaning to the information that they transmit. They give us this meaning through "thought," and they are responsible for every single pattern of thoughts we've ever had—from knowing how to skip down my street in Brooklyn, to processing what a clay bowl feels like as I'm shaping it in my palms, to understanding love and loyalty. We essentially all start with a blank slate when we're babies and generally have the same capacity for neural pathway creation.

When you think of something for the first time, such as taking your first step, the neurons in your brain light up, and the connections start a delicate and tender new pathway in your brain. It feels tough, as though it requires a much larger amount of energy, because it's new. But then, as you practice walking more, your neural pattern gets more established, and the neural pathway gets stronger and more stable. And soon, you're able to walk without consciously thinking about it. This is why, when my friend got into a horrible bike crash and badly injured her leg and couldn't walk, she had to learn how to walk again in physical therapy. Because she hadn't learned how to walk with this injury before, those neural pathways were entirely new for her. She had to go back to physical therapy many times a week and practice movements each day on her own to strengthen this new neural pathway, until she was able to get to a point where she could walk again with minimal conscious effort.

If we encounter a new thought but then never put that thought into practice again—if my friend had gone to physical therapy only once and had never returned—that new neural pathway connection is lost. We have to use our new "skill," or our brain will actually physically erase and disconnect from it in around twenty-four hours. So if we aren't thinking about or practicing our self-improvement each day until it is firmly established, it will be like starting from scratch each time (which is one of the reasons daily mantras are very helpful for shifting your perspective and creating new pathways of thought in your mind).

Neural pathways get super interesting when it comes to thought patterns that are tied to emotions. For example, if the first time you engaged with a dog as a child, the dog really scared you, you might go through your entire life with an emotional response of fear being linked to that neural pathway, as well as a personal narrative that dogs are scary. The "dogs are scary" narrative is now part of your identity, or the story that you tell yourself and others about who you are. You might even share frequently to others that you hate dogs as a subconscious conversation starter and receive a certain amount of surprise and attention each time, something that makes you feel unique or sets you apart from others.

When we're younger, our brains are much more "flexible," changing naturally and more easily in response to large or dramatic shifts. But once we hit adulthood, our brain forms these new neural pathways less frequently (we typically don't encounter as many new experiences as we did when we were learning how to be a human in the world); for this reason, many adults seem to have a much harder time changing than younger people do and may have outdated opinions that feel more "set in stone." The issue is that so much of who we are, or who we've decided ourselves to be, is based on outdated neural pathways that we don't necessarily need to be carrying around with us anymore. For example, if I grew up being told that I was too sensitive, then I'm going to have an adverse reaction to myself anytime I feel emotional. So I might learn to associate crying with weakness and become very critical of myself (and probably of others, too) whenever I (or they) need to cry, which is very harmful, because allowing yourself to feel and release emotions is key to self-regulation. For another example, if I have an early association with my father saying that he loved me and then beating me as a punishment when I did something wrong, and between blows exclaiming that he was "doing this for my own good," I might associate care and love with physical abuse, believing that when someone puts their hands on me, despite it feeling scary and intuitively wrong, they're ultimately doing it to help or protect me from myself. (That's a true story and a real association that I had in my brain up until around five years ago. And it's one *hell* of a neural pathway to adjust.)

My autistic experience is interesting when considering outdated neural pathways, because my brain often reacts adversely to things, such as metal cups, high-pitched voices, and slimy foods (like okra or cactus), in a way that doesn't seem to make much sense or to be in response to any negative associations with those things. My acupuncturist (a magical healer for whom I have immense respect and gratitude) once said that it's just that I have a lower threshold for the world. I have a higher threshold in many capacities, such as with my depth of feeling or ability to empathize, but a lower threshold when it comes to external stimuli. With my neurons firing away a lot more actively than a neurotypical brain (according to brain scans), my brain is constantly overprocessing and creating neural pathways that I don't even necessarily want it to have. So learning about neuroplasticity has been crucial in providing some hope for a bit of "retraining" of this chaos in my head, instead of just allowing myself to be perpetually swept away in the waves of it.

Yes, neural pathways can form associations with negative emotional responses and are very powerful in determining our behavior. But the field of neuroplasticity shows us that our neural pathways can actually *be changed*. "The language we use to describe the brain and how it operates—wires, circuits, networks, compartments, and so on—reflects a lingering idea that the brain is a somewhat rigid instrument," says Joe Dispenza, author of *Evolve Your Brain*. He continues:

> We often use the expression, "I've changed my mind." Until recently, science hasn't supported the contention that this change is a literal possibility. Only in the last thirty years or so has research revealed demonstrable proof that the adult brain continues to grow and change, forming new synaptic connections and severing others.... Now we know that we are able to change not only our mind, but also our brain. We can do this throughout our life and at will.

Neuroplasticity describes the characteristic that allows our brain to actually change and reorganize its synaptic wiring, or the way that it processes and applies the information it learns from its surrounding environment. And I am no scientist, but this data coming out (especially over the past twenty or so years) has been thoroughly exciting to me, because it proves that you can actually transform the neural pathways in your brain. We've been doing so since the beginning of time (which is how we have evolved as a species), but there is now actual proof that we can apply what we've observed, experienced, and learned in our lives to create different future experiences for ourselves. So when people say, "I can't help who I am attracted to," "This is just what I'm good at," or "This is just who I am," I now know that those statements are not entirely true. You actually have more control over your mind than you think you do.

According to an article by Tara Swart in *Forbes*, "encouraging the brain's neuroplasticity is the key to sustained adult learning and emotional intelligence, which will help the brain remain open-minded, intuitive and able to overcome biases throughout adulthood." Neuroscience has provided data showing that when you engage regularly in various practices that increase your feelings of happiness, awe, gratitude, and well-being, you strengthen this neural pathway activity, which then makes it easier to experience those feelings again, regardless of other mental health obstacles. Experts at the National Institutes of Health even believe that certain mental health symptoms, such as those associated with depression or anxiety, can benefit from a neuroplasticity repair process. Exercises that promote positive neuroplasticity may help to rewrite your neural pathways to ultimately improve your well-being overall.

And what's even more exciting is that you don't need a special skill to know how to do this, because you've been doing it all along, since you were a baby! You're constantly receiving new information throughout your life; you just have to decide if you will be receptive to receiving the new information; down to question your old story; and open to moving forward with a new, changed idea about a familiar situation. The first time my girlfriend Cristine came over to my house, she was amazed at how many plants I had: "Wow! I can't believe you can keep all of these alive. It seems like so much hard work. I can't even have one plant, because I'd kill it." From this statement, it was clear to me that she was limiting her potential plant joy based on a narrative she had decided on about herself. I don't know where it came from, and she probably didn't either. It was probably some outdated neural pathway that associated owning a plant with fear of not doing a good job taking care of it. And it was probably no longer relevant. So I just encouraged her to try a plant that's easy to take care of, like a snake plant, and start from there. She now has close to a hundred plants, her apartment looks like a rain forest, and she posts tips about plant care on her Instagram account all of the time. Because she was able to question her self-story and release it, she gave herself another chance at plant parenting and has now created a new self-narrative (and Instagram brand) associated with her updated neural pathway.

We all know how much trauma changes the brain and informs how we live our lives, but healing the brain and reparative energy work make a huge difference for our lives, too. However, it's not all easy: most neural pathways that involve deeper traumas take a lot more time to adjust and rework. Different scientists have been debating for years how long it actually takes to change a neural pathway and have concluded that it's different for every person. Some people can change their habits in just a few days, with what my partner Ryann and I refer to as a "hard pivot"; for others (likely more energetically fixed individuals), such changes can take up to a few years. In a study published in the *European Journal of Social Psychology*, Phillippa Lally, a health psychology researcher at University College London, and her research team concluded that it takes anywhere from 18 to 254 days for people to form a new habit, and 66 additional days for a new behavior to become automatic. Overall, scientists agree that the main way to enact the change is through repetition and focused, intentional concentration (that is, what you pay attention to will grow).

A NEW PRACTICE

I also like to consider: "What am I in practice of?" My friend Naima and I were sitting on my Brooklyn terrace this past summer eating a big salad that I served us for lunch, talking about a friend who was at a point in their life where they didn't seem happy with any of their choices, but also didn't know what to do about it. They were in a marriage that felt comfortable but not fulfilling, were working a job that felt stable but that wasn't aligned with what they wanted to be doing, and were about to have kids because their partner wanted to. I observed and shared that it seemed like *they never got the thing that they actually wanted*, and Naima confirmed this pattern after reflecting on what she had observed since becoming friends with this person in high school. I then shared my theory that they were simply *out of practice* with making risky decisions for themselves. Think about it: if when you are younger, you make your first very vulnerable and slightly risky decision for yourself and get rewarded for it or get the thing you want, you are positively reinforced to make another similar decision. Your whole life soon becomes a cycle of being able to recognize when it's time to shift, and time to make another decision that might feel risky and shake things up, but ultimately will most likely be rewarding for your life. But if you are negatively reinforced when you make your first, second, or third risky decision, you instead get into a pattern of regretting your decisions and sticking to what is already happening, what feels safe and comfortable. Soon a fear around large and risky decision-making emerges that might feel insurmountable. But really, you can decide to change the course of your life at any point of your life. If you feel like you're out of practice, talk to folks who you admire and who make rewarding risky decisions, or a life coach or therapist. Weigh the logical pros and cons, giving yourself permission to feel some discomfort and nervousness. Begin (or reclaim) a practice of trust-falling *with yourself*.

HOW TO SET UP YOUR LIFE

I'm not advocating that you fight against your brain your entire life. In fact, the supportive energy I've received from the world comes most often when I'm in a flow state, instead of in resistance to something (or in resistance to myself). But I do advocate setting your life up in a way that allows for your success to flow naturally and with ease. So, for example, if you're naturally inclined to spend large amounts of time on monomaniacal tasks, like knitting or practicing the piano—great! If that's not something that feels harmful, it doesn't make sense to put yourself in a work or life environment that includes many brief and changing projects if you prefer to dive into something more all-consuming. Instead, choose a work practice that exercises and celebrates your innate gifts, instead of putting yourself in situations where those gifts are underused and likely underappreciated.

I am also advocating setting your life up in a way that gives you permission to change, that allows you to adjust when you feel that things aren't working out. If you want to be nicer in your relationship with your partner, then work to change those neural pathways that have you jumping to snappy defensiveness when they share their feelings. Yes, the "work" often involves multiple months of deep self-assessment to figure out why you immediately get defensive when someone has feelings to share, but once you decide you want to change that response and work repetitively and intentionally to do so, you can. You can be more of anything that you decide you want to be.

In another example, if you find yourself thinking all the time that people are mad at you, then instead of just sticking to this story, try approaching your narrative with the openness of it having potential to change. Does something about this narrative feel safe to you? Does it represent how you felt as a child, and even though it's no longer relevant, you're holding onto it because it feels comfortable? Does having this narrative make you feel like a victim and thus give you permission to numb out or cry or drink too much? What are the things you feel you actually need in order to let go of this narrative? Maybe you need a couple weeks of disconnecting from social media, or extra rest, or maybe you need more affirmation from those who love you? All of those things can be arranged with an adjustment of your schedule and honest communication with others.

This isn't to say that your old narratives won't resurface, because they absolutely will. Even though there is an upward trend overall, like healing, change doesn't happen linearly. There will be days when your mind will feel clear and bright and you will be proud of yourself, and days when the voice in your head is screaming that you're not worth it. So you'll be at dinner with your friends, something will be said, and the little voice in your head will pop in with your comfort story: "You know they seem kind of mad at you. Maybe you did something wrong." But now that you've acknowledged that this story isn't real or relevant anymore, and you have new tools for approaching it, you can instead just ask, "Are you mad at me? Have I done something to offend you?" The answer will either be yes, in which case you can all have an open conversation about it and move forward, or it will be no, and you can release the nagging pull of that thought. Either way, being open and communicative about it is beneficial for your healing and for changing the pathways in your brain. You get one step closer to a more honest relationship with yourself when you acknowledge what plagues you and what makes you feel vulnerable, out loud. And this sharing is ultimately one of the most powerful ways to connect and grow in relationship with someone you care about.

CHILDHOOD NARRATIVES

Even what our guardians and teachers called us as children builds out our self-story. Were you always first in line? Too bossy? Too hyper and "hard to deal with" (aka control)? What narratives did you learn about yourself as a young person that you can now release? What were you identified as when you were younger that is actually inhibiting your growth as an adult? My whole childhood and adolescence, my parents raised me with the tale that I was sensitive, special, and gifted, yes, but never with the idea that I had a disability. Whenever I had trouble focusing in school, couldn't study outside of school, had a lot of difficulty taking tests, or felt too much anxiety participating in class the entire semester, my dad would tell me that there were other pathways to getting things done (and "getting things done," in this case, was getting at least a B for the semester). He would tell me that I could create another structure that worked for me to achieve the same goal, like instead of participating in class, I could ask the teacher for an additional project to do.

I was taught from a young age that there was always an opportunity when there was an obstacle in front of me. As much as I appreciate this perspective, because it got me to Georgetown University and Wall Street and running multiple successful businesses, it also meant that many of my autism discoveries have come later in my life. I am finally creating new neural pathways and learning (and am still learning every day) about how stimming can be very beneficial to my energetic release; the types of environments I need to feel well balanced and safe (definitely not working at a bank, being in a restrictive relationship, or living in a maximalist space), and the types of support I need to maintain loving friendships and relationships (that is, tons of direct communication). My identification as someone who could endure anything, work in any environment, and always "be fine" was not actually the truth of who I am, but I didn't know anything else because I had internalized my dad's narrative of perfectionism and being easy to parent, teach, and work with. This was evident in the frequent panic attacks I was having; the blackouts and physically destructive rages I would go through when I drank; and the deep sadness that would bubble up occasionally where I would stim (without knowing what that was), sob for hours on end, cut myself, and then finally feel reset enough to mask and give people what they expected of me. Choosing who you want to be is as much about choosing your own story as it is about finding your innate gifts, the underlying truth of yourself that was there all along, visible only once you pull away your masks.

MAKING CHANGES

Some of the neural pathways that I have been working to change most recently are my narratives about my autistic brain being a weakness or an issue that I have to contend with, rather than a unique and special way of being that actually is brimming with gifts that many neurotypical people don't have. I'm working on forming new pathways with regard to receiving love and care, reminding myself frequently that asking for and receiving support is also a crucial part of a friendship exchange. Coming from a household in which rest was a reward for hard work, and physical affection and good moods came only on holidays, I also work to remind myself frequently that I am deserving of rest and affection and joy *always*. Through this work, my self-story now includes that I am deeply sensitive (and it's a great thing), kinky and sexually perverse (moving past my prior narrative of believing that sex should be enjoyed only in one format and in ways that were respectable), autistic(ally gifted), and that I need a lot of rest, alone time, and solid boundaries to feel my best.

I also love creating mental reward systems as I grow. One of my past resolutions for a new year was that I want to do more activities that affirm the life I envision for myself. So anytime I do an activity that does, I'll affirm myself for it (out loud) and then take a moment to visualize again the life that I envision for myself. This self-affirmation decreases my cortisol levels and allows my serotonin to increase, which then creates an immediately felt positive reward. The more I do things that support the life I envision for myself, the more I get rewarded in my creation of it.

Run yourself through the following exercise often (and also see Chapter 3: "Question Everything"): Do I like what's happening in my life right now? What would I change? Who do I want to be that I'm not? Should I drop every single thing and move across the world to start an entirely new life (lol jk, kinda)? Visualize your life as something completely different. Visualize yourself as the person you want to be. How are people responding to you? How are you experiencing hardship or challenges or setbacks? Do you claim you want freedom but actually fear the lack of structure that your freedom might bring? Why?

Ask yourself what aspects of this new life you want to incorporate into your life now and then make a plan to take a small tangible step each day to begin incorporating those things.

Knowing that I have flexibility, and actually considering the changes in real time and often, help me feel I'm actively choosing the life I live each day. I'm choosing who and how I want to be. This helps me feel free.

When I was younger, I kept looping on a quote that I saw on one of those square "inspiring quote" magnets that you can find on the twirling displays in gift shops: "Shoot for the moon, because even if you miss, you'll land among the stars." This corny magnet has influenced my way of thinking more than I care to admit—because it's true! Our minds are powerful and the placebo effect is real! If I (someone with diagnosed ADHD as a comorbid symptom of my autism) decide that I'm great at focusing, I will do a better job at focusing than if I decide I'm horrible at focusing. So why not decide what you want in your life? Even if you don't get all the way there, you'll still be steps closer than the version of yourself who decided your life was already all planned out and your weaknesses decided on. Why not open yourself to inspiration or, at the least, a small and different choice today that might eventually inspire other openings within and around you?

MY AGENCY TO CHOOSE
by Tourmaline

Early in the pandemic, I got coffee with Becca McCharen Tran in Brooklyn to discuss what would later become our Chromat x Tourmaline swimsuit line, Collective Opulence Celebrating Kindred. I remember entering the park on the rainy spring day and Becca greeting me with bagels, and feeling fully alive with an idea of designing swimwear that to my knowledge never has existed before, suits that included designs for swimwear for girls who don't tuck, trans femmes, nonbinary and trans masc people who pack, intersex babes, women, men, and everyone embracing Collective Opulence Celebrating Kindred.

Why was this important? To me it was (and is) about cultivating a landscape where all of who we are gets to show up in any given moment; it meant that transness gets to expand and be embodied beyond anyone saying what "the right way to be" is. It meant the ongoing unfolding of Chromat's mission to make space for all of us to take up space on the beach, by the pool, or in our bedrooms. I can't think of anything more sexy than being fully alive, and that first meeting was electric with that innovative energy.

More than a year later, we got to debut the collection at Riis Beach, a home for the queer and trans community on New York City's Rockaway Peninsula, where I've been going since 2005. I felt awestruck that this thought had swiftly and beautifully turned into a manifested, tangible thing, something that many were excited to wear up and down the boardwalk, that fashion photographers were taking photos of, and that journalists were writing about. I can't overstate how fun it was to get in the water with all the models and splash around like the Cancer queen I am in fits that were, only a little while before, a vision living in my head. This moment represented being uniquely who I am—and *that I have the agency to choose who that is* and invite my community into experiencing that pleasurable feeling for ourselves.

TOURMALINE (she/her) is June 2022's winner of Art Basel's biggest prize and her work lives in the permanent collection of every major museum in NYC + beyond. Her self-portraits are centerpieces of the new Afrofuturist Period Room of the Met, unveiled in early 2022. She is currently writing the official biography of Marsha P. Johnson (Tiny Reparations/Penguin Random House, 2024). Her work is on view right now at the 59th Venice Biennale; she dropped her first clothing collection with Chromat in 2021, a first-of-its-kind bathing suit line for trans girls who don't tuck; she was a TIME 100 Most Influential Person awardee (2020); she's made Dove's Pride campaigns for the last three years and counting; she's a Guggenheim fellow; and an activist for the past decade—changing NYC laws around the targeting of and discrimination against trans and gender nonconforming people. Her work explores ethics and pleasure, foregrounding the beauty of deviance and the possibilities of collective and opulent dreaming. She highlights and centers, always, the transmutational experiences and groundbreaking aesthetics of Black, queer, and trans communities, and their deep capacity to impact the world. From limiting conditions she dreams and executes limitless things.

SEVEN

Use Your Fear and Your Rage

I realize that if I wait until I am no longer afraid to act, write, speak, be, I'll be sending messages on a Ouija board, cryptic comments from the other side. When I dare to be powerful, to use my strength in the service of my vision, then it becomes less important whether or not I am unafraid.

—AUDRE LORDE, *THE CANCER JOURNALS*

FEAR IS AN ENORMOUS PART OF MY DAILY EXPERIENCE. AS A BLACK & Indigenous, femme, queer woman living in a world where people still have very open and vehement oppositions to my lived existence, fear is a baseline feeling that sits in my bones. It intermingles with my intuition and guides which route I take home, to whom and how I respond when catcalled as I'm walking down the street to the grocery store, and where I choose to travel internationally with my partner. And most people don't know this, but as an autistic person, fear permeates every millimeter of me, filling my veins with a pulsing charge that might spark and ignite at any moment.

I am fearful of interacting with people, fearful of smells and particles and things sticking to my hands, fearful of loud noises and flashing lights, fearful of all that I might not be prepared for experiencing at any moment that might overwhelm me and plunge me into a meltdown. I am fearful of leaving my apartment and sometimes even of being in my apartment. Because I was raised in a highly monitored household where I wasn't even allowed to close my door, I am fearful of being watched and fearful of being taken. The OCD and paranoia I experience as comorbid symptoms of my autism make it very difficult to exist in my body, because the fear of most things outside of my control typically leads to a crippling and exhausting anxiety that I have to push through in order to exist in this world, every. single. day. Even though I enjoy the world and this life and humans and desperately want to interact and connect and relate, I'm fearful because, at any moment, someone might get too close, or something might be way too sticky, or sounds and lights might be way too loud—and my mind will begin to fill with smog. Dark, thick molasses starts to creep through the ridges of my brain until my head feels heavy and I can't shake it out. I can do drugs or drink plenty of alcohol to free myself, but without those numbing agents, no matter how much I stim or rest or move, sometimes the smog just won't loosen its hold on me. My ears feel clogged, my eyes lose their sight, and all of the loud noise of my existence bubbles up inside of me until it erupts into a meltdown, finally allowing everything to reset.

Sometimes the fear takes over before I can even get outside for the day, and I can't leave the safety of my bed. But then other times, I can travel and talk to new people without numbing myself first. It all depends on whatever chemical concoction is happening in my brain on that given day. Each day is different, but every day is filled with self-coaching, mantras, and pushing through my fear in a distinctive and exhausting way.

Several years ago I had to undergo a small surgery in which a monitor was installed next to my heart. For a decade, cardiologists haven't been able to figure out why my heart seems to get overly excited in response to seemingly mundane situations, but then has difficulty rising to the occasion when I'm doing something active, like running on a treadmill. They haven't been able to find any solutions, so now have resolved to just monitor me as I record my symptoms on my corresponding heart monitor phone app. But it all feels so clear to me that it's almost amusing: my heart is simply responding to the world around me the way that my brain does—she's overly sensitive and easily startled. She's ready with a fight-or-flight response to every situation, even (and sometimes especially) when it's just a new person approaching me with a comment about the weather.

Once I realized that my inherent fear-based reaction to everything wasn't something most other people experienced, I thought I was doomed. My fear felt like a clear signal to me that what was happening around me was wrong. If I let that dictate how I engaged with and interacted with the world, I would have no new experiences and no friendships, and I would never take any risks; things felt much safer in my bubble of routine and comfort, anyway. But then all the Gemini in my chart probably had a tantrum. And I started pushing myself to live outside of my comfort zone little by little. I mean, I had been doing that my whole life (mainly so that I could try my best to fit in with others in typical life circumstances that seemed normal and easy for everyone else to handle), but now I was *intentional* about it. Because I always feel scared and never feel ready, I've learned to push through those feelings and do the thing anyway. I intentionally chose to do things that I was afraid of and put myself in situations that I knew I had anxiety about, because I realized that these feelings, like all emotions and feelings, would pass. And once they did pass, would I want to still be in bed, or would I want to be in another country? Would I want to still be watching TV, or would I want to be supporting a friend's live music performance? Sometimes, the answer would be "Yes, I would still very much want to be in bed" (because we stan rest!—see Chapter 1: "Fuck Being Busy"). But when I'm able to identify that what is holding me back is fear or anxiety, then I can intentionally choose to "do the thing" anyway. This doesn't mean that I'm not prepared with my noise-canceling headphones, my light-blocking shades, and in the winter my puffy coat and big scarf for sensory protection, but it does mean that I can *give myself permission to experience the world*, even if it is in my own unique way.

THE DECISION-MAKING PROCESS

For each person, the fears, anxieties, and coping strategies can look completely different. But what does it look like to identify and separate your fear-based feelings from your desire, so that you can really examine the desire on its own to determine whether following it is the right choice for you? For many of us, fear can never be fully removed from the picture. But what does your life look like, and how does a world of opportunity open up around you, if fear can be intentionally removed from your decision-making process?

In her 2018 TED talk "Get Comfortable with Being Uncomfortable," Luvvie Ajayi Jones talks about how the current systems of oppression count on our silence so that we can stay where we are. They count on our fear: fear of speaking up, fear of being a disrupter, fear of losing what we already have—wanting us to internalize "What will I lose?" instead of "What do I have to gain?" So when I am fearful or anxious, I often ask myself, what or whom is my fear or anxiety serving? If it isn't protecting me and telling me I need to take things slower and that I need rest, then for what reasons am I honoring it? For what reasons am I prioritizing it and allowing it to inhibit my actions moving forward? If my life goal ultimately is to fulfill my truest expression of myself as a human being, or as Oprah put it in her 2012 commencement address at Spellman College, to "fulfill the promise that the Creator dreamed when he dreamed the cells that made up me," then even if I'm not sure of the future vision, is my fear serving the ultimate expression of my self? What does it look like to sit with this fear, acknowledge it, and let it pass? And if it doesn't pass, what does it look like to acknowledge it but not choose to dwell in it? Carl Jung once said that "everyone carries a shadow and the less it is embodied in the individual's conscious life, the denser it is." Learn how to recognize, identify, and play with fear as a natural part of yourself, like your shadow self, rather than fighting it. Learn how to sit with the discomfort of those feelings. Only then will they become easier to move through.

In Jason Reynolds's guest segment on *The Washington Post*'s *Race in America* series, he says,

> *I never would have became the person that I've become if it weren't for my uncomfortable moments .... I think discomfort is the springboard into possibility, right, and to the opportunity to*

be better, to be whole, to complicate our own arguments, right? ... [It allows us] to wrestle with the things that we think we believe, to actually shake the ground in which we walk on, which is a frightening thing sometimes, but it doesn't actually mean that you're in any physical danger ... Like, those words "uncomfortable" and "unsafe" are different for a reason, right? And then if you allow yourself to be uncomfortable a little more often, then somebody else might be physically safer, might be made physically safer because of your allowance of your discomfort.

Often, our inaction won't necessarily make us more safe, but the courage of our action might actually create safe spaces for others who still fear their action, too.

ANGER AND RAGE

Anger and rage are several steps beyond fear—but are also natural reactions to living in such an, at times, inhumane and cruel world. Our rage communicates that what is happening around us is not okay. For much of my twenties, I felt most alive only when I was channeling the intensity of rage. Rage is wild, and it is useful. It encourages actionable change when used productively, and it should not be suppressed or minimized or silenced. Resmaa Menakem, a therapist and trauma specialist, even argues that how we've experienced collective trauma is what goes into how we relate to others and what we identify as our community's culture:

> For my Black body to be born into a society by which the white body is the standard is, in and of itself, traumatizing. If my mom is born as a Black woman, into a society that predicates her body as deviant, the amount of cortisol that is in her nervous system when I'm being born is teaching my nervous system something. Trauma decontextualized in a person looks like personality. Trauma decontextualized in a family looks like family traits. Trauma in a people looks like culture.

So without even consciously knowing it most of the time, we hold our responses to this trauma (our fear, our anger, and our rage) in both our individual bodies and our collective pain body, potentially even spanning across fourteen generations.

Despite the prevalence of rage and its effect on all of us, it's also something, like fear, that we all seem to actively try to avoid. We deem anger and rage as "bad," but what if, as with fear, we can begin to recognize and hold rage with care? Or even use it—as a tool, an offering, a portal?

Thich Nhat Hanh, during a May 2014 retreat at Plum Village, the monastic community he founded in southwest France, answered questions from the young people in the audience.

One of them asked, "When I get angry, how do I let my anger out?" He responded with a comparison:

> *Anger is not something pleasant. It's like the mud. But without the mud, we cannot grow lotus flowers. So the mud is useful somehow, so your anger is useful somehow. So, maybe you should not let it out. You should not throw it away. If you know how to make good use of your anger, you can grow the lotus of peace, of joy, of forgiveness. This is a very deep teaching.*
>
> *Anger comes up not from the outside, but from the inside. If we look deeply, if we listen deeply, we'll be able to understand. When we understand there is love, and then anger transforms itself . . . . If you hold that anger in understanding, in compassion, then anger becomes something like love.*

BLACK RAGE

In the online magazine *Sojourners*, writer and speaker Danté Stewart explains:

> *Black rage in an anti-Black world is a spiritual virtue. Rage shakes us out of our illusion that the world as it is, is what God wants. Rage forces us to deal with the gross system of inequality, exploitation, and disrespect . . . . Rage is the work of love that*

stands against an unloving world. If you're more concerned about the responses of Black rage than you are about a system that justifies and rewards Black death, you don't love Black people—you just love when they stay in their place. And that's not love, that's hate.

Rage is a natural response to the ongoing violence that so many of us experience every day. It's here and present and makes sense. And *we need it*. But unchecked rage performs like acid: too much of it simmering and brewing in our system will slowly and internally burn us alive.

Journalist and author Krista Tippett references this in her podcast episode with Jason Reynolds, when they talk about the difference between "reactionary rage" and "conscious rage." He says,

Black folks have a right to have a conscious rage. I mean, Baldwin always talks about it. If you are a Black person who is conscious in America, then you are basically living in a state of anger . . . . The other thing I will say . . . and not as a pushback but as an addendum, is that if it is not a conscious rage—meaning, if it is not a rage that we can tap into, a rage that exists within the quiver of our lives, along with the joy—then it can very well poison us and overtake us. And it can become an illness . . . . So reactionary rage is a dangerous thing. But to be able to tap into a conscious rage, I think, is a gift. And I do believe it is a virtue.

Some people argue that the opposite of joy is rage. But I would say that rage isn't oppositional to joy, because out of a conscious rage can come creation. When we're able to tap into our informed and conscious rage, we can use it as an energetic resource, a well from which we can pull our inspiration, our activism, our joy, and even our pleasure.

I also think a lot about what author and activist Mia Birdsong says in her book *How We Show Up*:

Managing the impact of external and internalized oppression is both something I'm used to and something that exhausts and breaks my heart. It's a lot . . . . Not only is [it] not easy and not our fault, it's not fair. It's not fair that we inherit all this baggage, but . . . shit is not fair. We can certainly rail against what is unfair . . . and fight against injustice. But at the end of the day, we—each one of us—are the only ones who can decide we are going to suffer less in the face of the wrongs we have experienced and continue to experience. We can decide that our own experience of contentment, pleasure, and liberation is ultimately more important than being pissed about the fact that we shouldn't have to deal with it in the first place.

I'm reminded in reading this about a small hope in the midst of the pain—that I have agency over my perspective and thus (even if only gradually) over my circumstances. And how do we care for ourselves (because, as Audre Lorde said, caring for ourselves is self-preservation, not self-indulgence) in the midst of our fear, our anger, and our rage (that is, our consciousness) so that they do not consume us? How do we imagine a world beyond our present one and use our rage to ignite us into action?

Sourced from their rage in response to an unjust education system, my close friend Ki founded Woke Kindergarten, a global abolitionist community of unlearning, as a way to "share knowledge that galvanizes the littlest of us to resist, abolish, create and liberate." Through their platform, they share "Woke Read Alouds," host anti-racist and anti-bias curriculum training for schools, and more, and their community now has close to sixty thousand members, encouraging young people to freedom-dream their ways into liberatory futures.

Ellen Bass starts her poem "The Thing Is": "to love life, to love it even / when you have no stomach for it / and everything you've held dear / crumbles like burned paper in your hands . . ." How can we endure all that we've endured so far? But then "you hold life like a face . . . and you say, yes, I will take you / I will love you, again." Perhaps, when we, for generations, have been so forcibly broken, the only way through is to keep moving—to choose to keep caring for ourselves, and each other, through pleasure activism, celebration, and joy.

In 2017, bell hooks and Thich Nhat Hanh met together to dialogue about how to build a community of love. They talked about having a right to anger and that only by *considering it* can it be transformed into understanding, compassion, and love:

> *It is with negative energy that you can make the positive energy. A flower, although beautiful, will become compost someday, but if you know how to transform the compost back into the flower, then you don't have to worry. You don't have to worry about your anger because you know how to handle it—to embrace, to recognize, and to transform it. So this is what is possible.*

The first law of thermodynamics says that energy can be changed from one form to another, but it cannot be created or destroyed. With no judgment, I watch a lot of folks in my communities use their pain, trauma, fear, and rage as a drain rather than as a source. And it makes sense—after fighting so hard just to exist, what strength do we have to repurpose and reintegrate the rage-filled energy that we're experiencing? Sometimes our focus on the pain then becomes an outlet for our self-sabotage, which then ends up stifling us more than the actual circumstances might have. Each of us individually can choose how to use our fear and how to use our rage. All energy can be transmuted and transformed with the proper direction. From the Black Lives Matter movement, to anti-Black racism training, to anti-racism philanthropic efforts, to the #MeToo movement—when we're able to see our pain, sit with it, feel it, and transform our fear and rage into creative outlets, what results are some of the most powerfully revitalizing tools for our community. Even if the responsibility of doing something big feels too heavy, too exhausting a burden, we can take a minute for our breath, a nap, a moment to see, in the midst of all of this destruction and disease and love starvation (because they do exist—and still), how deeply abundant and beautiful the miracle of your life is, even if just for this moment.

Writer and performance artist Sharon Bridgforth said, "Even when you can't see it / reach for love again and again and again. / Know that your love / is more powerful than your rage."

A THOUGHT MEDITATION IN FEELING WHAT'S DIFFICULT
by Fariha Róisín

How often are we told to *not* weaponize but, instead, to sublimate rage, to use it like a ball of energy straight out of Dragon Ball Z, to use it as a superpower? Many of us are riddled with anger, yet we are told that the world we live in—the current sinister reality of mass destruction, mass poverty, and mass disconnection from one another and the Earth—is not enough for revolution. We are told things are fine, passable. Yet so many know this isn't true and thus have grown weary, our anger neutralized through the pursuit of capitalism and mundane pleasure. But what of the purity of the throttling rage? That feeling of fire shooting through your body, electric. It's still there even when you diffuse it. Underneath it all, it is coiled up, waiting for you to acknowledge it.

So you may ask, "What do I do, then, Fariha?" And I hear you. Not everyone can (or wants to) unleash their rage—but imagine using it for something profound, such as justice. Instead of becoming a part of the problem, how can we make sure that the spiritual fight of liberation is never forgotten in any action? How can we sustain the fire that is required and turn it toward service?

For me, personally, spiritual warfare has taken over my soul. The anger I feel for the Earth, for the destruction of it—the more I feel it, the more I channel it into my work, into how I interact with others and my community. So feel into the feeling and think of active ways you could use that beautiful, erotic energy known as rage. What can it be funneled into? Perhaps into art, music, organizing, or community gardening and peer mentoring—into a ripe sense of responsibility.

Whatever you do, use your rage for revolution.

FARIHA RÓISÍN (she/they) is a multidisciplinary artist born in Ontario, Canada. She was raised in Sydney, Australia, and is based in Brooklyn, New York. As a Muslim queer Bangladeshi, she is interested in the margins, liminality, otherness, and the mercurial nature of being. Her work has pioneered a refreshing and renewed conversation about wellness, contemporary Islam, and queer identities and has been featured in the *New York Times, Al Jazeera, The Guardian, and Vogue*. She is the author of the poetry collection *How To Cure a Ghost* (2019) and the novel *Like a Bird* (2020). Her latest work is a book of nonfiction entitled *Who Is Wellness For?* (2022). Her second book of poetry is entitled *Survival Takes a Wild Imagination*. She can be found at @fariha_roisin.

EIGHT

Queer Your Friendships

Queer not as being about who you're having sex with (that can be a dimension of it); but queer as being about the self that is at odds with everything around it and has to invent and create and find a place to speak and to thrive and to live.

—BELL HOOKS, "PUBLIC DIALOGUE AT THE NEW SCHOOL"

GROWING UP, I ALWAYS FELT LIKE I IDENTIFIED MORE WITH "THE boys," the simpler group of friends on my block who, instead of conducting indoor tea parties with warm soy milk like the girls, wanted to be outside running up and down the street doing cartwheels, jumping on the pogo stick, and challenging each other to obstacle course races. The tea parties involved a lot of small talk and intimate socializing whereas the outdoor rough-housing might involve a skinned knee (and even then, I was a masochist—collecting my scars like badges). As I grew up, it was hard for me to relate to friends intimately. I held people at an arm's distance to protect myself, building friendships centered only on going out, joking around, and being active (and having fun!) together in the world, instead of thinking of friendships as a resource that could support me, fill me, and teach me things about myself. That kind of friendship, I felt, was reserved for my queer lovers—my array of boyfriends, girlfriends, and boifriends on whom I would intimately rely for all things emotional and vulnerable.

It felt so much easier for me to reserve my more "cool" and "in control" parts of my personality for my friends, people I didn't actually allow to see me fully, and let only a select few people into the depths of me. I felt too intense, too weird, too socially awkward (unless I was masking and presenting this "cool" and "stoic" face or numbing myself through drinking and drugs); I genuinely felt I was actually saving my friends time and energy by giving them only what I perceived to be the "best" parts of me. And, wow, was I wrong! I pushed away countless friends, shutting down and removing myself when things became anything other than easy and fun. And I often told my partners that I "didn't actually care" about anyone else other than them. I could barely even let my friends touch me until college—being autistic and uncomfortable with initiating physical intimacy and also having grown up in a house with very little hugging or familial intimacy, confused about what kinds of physical touch and affection should be reserved only for people I was sexually involved with and romantically dating.

When I arrived in Brooklyn after moving from the East Village, I was eager to finally be living full-time around the radical group of queer artists and activists I'd been spending all of my weekends around. I started being exposed to ways of thinking and living that I hadn't considered or seen modeled elsewhere, experiencing folks who were living their lives based on new frameworks that they created, which I never realized were possible or "allowed"—such as several queer adult artists, some with live-in families too, creating a communal living structure in which they hosted events and shared responsibilities of upkeep for the large mansion that they all lived in together. Or a single gay writer, wanting to have a baby but not a sexual partner, so choosing to get pregnant instead with the help of the community of coparents she enlisted for support. Or two adult women choosing to live together instead of with their romantic partners, referring to themselves as each other's wives, and very much treating their home space as folks in a traditional, heteronormative marriage would treat their space—picking furniture together, sharing expenses, hosting seasonal brunches and cookie-decorating nights to celebrate the holidays with their families. Being in Brooklyn and surrounding myself with this community had me expanding in ways I hadn't considered—questioning what family, home, partnership, community, and friendship could actually look like, and what roles I wanted these relationships to play in my life.

I began to dig deeper: Why did I reserve intimacy, vulnerability, and romance for only my sexual partners? How could I feel safe and supported with a friend in the same way that I did with a sexual partner? What pressures were I putting on my sexual partners to provide and be everything for me, and how was that affecting our relationships? Why was I viewing friendship and romance on opposite ends of a binary spectrum?

In relationship therapist Esther Perel's 2014 conversation with NPR, she said,

> We want our partner to still give us all these things [a partnership for life in terms of children, social status, and companionship], but in addition, I want you to be my best friend and my trusted confidant and my passionate lover to boot . . . we come to one person, and we basically are asking them to give us what once an entire village used to provide.

And if we're putting all this pressure on one person to be all of these things, what depth and possibility am I missing out on in my other relationships? How can I apply the concept of "queerness" (as it relates to questioning everything, to redefining and embracing what works for me, to challenging the sociopolitical structures that have dictated how I experience the world) to my friendships?

Almost a decade later, friendship now for me feels like freedom. It feels like open space: space that I can make up as I journey deeper into it, where I can workshop my decisions, communicate my needs, be generous, take risks, express my hurt feelings, rise to the occasion, cry, be uplifted, and feel held down. I've learned that bonds are strengthened by asking for what you need, by allowing my friends to show up for me.

A guilty-as-charged *Sex and the City* fan, I love what Carrie said to Miranda in the season 5 episode "Luck Be an Old Lady":

> *Friendships don't magically last forty years. You have to invest in them! It's like your savings: you don't expect to wake up one day when you're old and find a big bucket of money waiting there. My point is, we need an emotional retirement plan. This is important, making time for each other and taking trips like this. Because as we can see here, at the end of the line, it's just going to be us ladies riding a bus.*

How do we invest in friendships to support our emotional retirement plan?

One late summer evening this past year, a few of my closest friends and I were crouched around an outdoor table at the Williamsburg restaurant Diner, after first indulging earlier in celebration oysters and bubbly down the street at Maison Premiere. We leaned forward and into one another, describing the romanticism and utter delight that our daylong date, and in general, that our friendship brings us. We talked about our commitment to one another and how that was prioritized in each of our lives. But I wanted to hear more! So I decided to host these friends again for brunch in my home. I made a roasted squash and garlic ricotta buckwheat galette; balsamic-roasted beets with a herb and orange zest gremolata; baked feta with a rosemary and blackberry compote; a mixed greens salad with lentils, a mustardy vinaigrette, and crispy onions; and a refreshingly herbal beet and lime spritz. We sat in the front room of my Brooklyn home, with Naima and I sprawled on my alpaca wool daybed, Ora and Jessie on floor poufs around the bouclé ottoman, and Giovanna dialing in from Los Angeles. What follows is the transcribed, minimally edited, incredibly moving conversation that we had that sleepy Sunday afternoon.

Sara Elise: First, I wanted to thank you for being here in my home, virtually and physically. I'm writing this chapter on queering friendship—and y'all are the reason that I'm writing this chapter. And it's too early to cry [*immediately proceeds to cry*], but I can't express my gratitude enough for your presence in my life. It's changed me very deeply. Thank you.

I wanted to host you, which I love doing, and welcome you into my home and my heart to have this discussion, because y'all are what queering friendship is about. I wanted to include you in this chapter because you are the reason that I'm in this place and the reason that I'm thinking about all of this and why I'm experiencing [such profound] friendship in this way.

The reason I'm writing this chapter is because friendship has always been such a [peculiar] thing to me. As you know, I'm autistic. And I've found that, when I'm masked, making quick, surface-level connections has been very easy for me. I'll be at a party, and now I have a new "friend," and that doesn't feel difficult to me [because when I'm out and masking, it feels easier to perform connection]. But doing the deep, intimate connective friendship- and community-building work is something that I really longed for my whole life but always felt difficult for me to access and then to stay grounded in, because I felt like I didn't have the tools to do that. And part of that is because of my family and upbringing: my parents seemingly never prioritized their friendships at all. I experienced them having only a few friends their entire lives, and they didn't seem to value their friendships. They were open to socializing and celebration, but if there was a conflict, my parents would just cut the person out of their life, and we wouldn't see them anymore. And we didn't know what the conflict was; it was just like, "We're not hanging out with them anymore." So I really thought that your romantic and sexual partner was the person you were "unmasked" with, the person you're open with who sees the real you. And then your friends just come and go, based on ease and fun and convenience.

I literally have only had one friend; you guys all met my friend from grade school—Sarah Grimm. Even through college, she's the only friend who I ever intentionally allowed to see me cry and see an "unmasked" version of myself. With everyone else, I had these "friendships" that were based on fun and going out and [connecting through] drugs. I felt really strongly about being able to control the narrative: so with [this group of] people, I would be this version of myself, and with [this group of] people, I perform this [version], but I would never let anyone in or actually get close to me unless they were a sexual or romantic partner, because that was my priority: that's what I'm building and that's where I'm deepening. So whenever things felt too vulnerable with friends, I would shut it down or make a joke or [end up eventually] pushing people away.

So because of my autism and my feeling like an outsider my whole life and because of my upbringing, it's felt very difficult for me to accept love or ask for help [*begins crying again*]. And I've just gone so much of my life trying to prove to myself that my strength could come in my self-sufficiency and that as long as I tended to my island and made my island really strong and on point, I didn't actually need anyone else to join me there.

So moving to Brooklyn and being exposed to y'all . . . has really changed me. And I've learned that friendship is a practice: a ritual of making again and again. It's a form of intimate connection that, yes, can feel exciting and fun and celebratory—but the growth and the deep transformation also comes when there's work and conflict and discomfort. It feels very vulnerable for me to be trusting y'all with my heart in this way, but so transformational. So that's why I'm writing this chapter, because I think it's such a powerful and transforming thing to experience this type of love and . . . I didn't know. I didn't know it existed.

So I just want other folks to really think about their defini-tion of friendship and think about their priority of their relationships—sexual or romantic partners, family rela-tionships, friendships—and how they prioritize and structure them in their lives. My whole book is about en-couraging people to reconsider their whole lives and how they've been taught to think about things. Luckily because I'm autistic, so much of my life I've been in conflict with what I've been taught because it doesn't fit for me. So be-cause of that gift, I think I'm able to have a unique per-spective in helping people to access that questioning for themselves.

So this chapter is about questioning friendship, the role it plays in your life, and thinking about how to queer what you thought about it.

[*Sara Elise holds up* How We Show Up *by Mia Birdsong.*]

In this book, [Mia] shares: "The word free is derived from the Indo-European *friya*, which means 'beloved'.) Friend also shares this common root with freedom. A free person was someone who was 'joined to a tribe of free people by ties of kinship and rights of belonging' (from David Hackett Fischer's *Liberty and Freedom: A Visual History of America's Founding Ideas*). Freedom was the idea that together we can ensure that we all have the things we need—love, food, shelter, safety. The way I've come to understand it, freedom is both an individual and collective endeavor—a multilayered process, not a state of being. Being free is, in part, achieved through being connected."

I really love thinking about that to begin our discussion. I'd love to hear folks' thoughts on how you view friendship in relationship to being connected. For me, I thought friendship was: "I can still be an island, and I can have friends." And that's what I've observed as friendship for so many people. But what do you think the importance of connection is for friendship, and in the grand scheme of being connected to people, where do you think friendship fits into that?

Gio: Thinking about care a lot and how care is what you put out, but also [it's] about if you're open to receiving as well. That's what allows for real connection. What you can put out and give is part of it—but also your vulnerability, your capacity to stay open, be open, be touched by said person, acknowledge the feeling, notice how it lands in you, experience all the feelings that may come (whether that's a harder feeling or an easier feeling to feel) is just as much a part of creating connection. And I think especially in friendships and relationships, that part is underplayed. There's not enough discussion around *you* being vulnerable, and you staying open, and you being open to touch in strengthening that connection. And that's something I'm definitely in process of learning with y'all and am moved to continue that work through being in relationship with y'all.

Ora: We feel you!

Sara Elise: Yes, we're all over here nodding in agreement.

Gio: I am driving and have one hand on the wheel and my other hand on my heart.

Naima: I really feel like my friends have always been my life. They've been the people who help inform who I am and how I change and the ways that I feel connected to myself. [But] sometimes the hardest thing for me to do is allow people to witness me when I'm not put together, or arriving here and I'm like, "I've cried four times today, but I'm fine!" I'm trying so hard to seem like I've got it together, but [I'm working on] allowing myself to come undone with friends and people who I really trust.

And something about my friendship with you, Sara Elise, is that I really trust that we're going to figure it out. Even if there's a miscommunication, there's just a deep commitment to both giving each other space and giving each other the love and generosity that "this is not coming from a malicious place," that there's the deep love and trust that we're trying to take care of each other. Deep friendship has always been such a priority, and sometimes has come second to my romantic relationships because I'm like, "but [my friends are] going to be here and you might not be." [I just always know] that no matter what, my friends would always be there for me and help me to work my way through and around and out in whatever way was needed.

Sara Elise: Thank you, Naima. So far I'm hearing about trust, care, and vulnerability. When I'm thinking of a queered friendship, I also think a lot about intimacy. I was watching this performance by a Black woman spoken word poet named Alisha Lockley, and she talks about how intimacy means falling. She imagines a diving, a self-unraveling that happens. "How beautiful is it to have someone, not necessarily a romantic partner or a lover, but just another human being that we can allow ourselves to be broken in front of. Having someone with which we are not afraid to be scared." So I was just interested in hearing your thoughts on what role you feel intimacy plays in a queered friendship and what that might look like for y'all in the context of our friendships.

Jessie: I think that for me, our friendship, and now I'm going to cry, but our friendship specifically, like with you, is the most sacred, meaningful, impactful work of my life. And it's been so difficult for me to feel vulnerable with people because I haven't felt safe. Growing up, I always felt like an island, too, and felt like I wouldn't be fully seen—and thus had to keep so much of my true self in this sacred internal compartment, because I didn't feel like it was safe to have that intimacy. And I just feel like we've been moving toward each other our whole lives, and all the experiences we've had or lack of intimacy in other kinds of friendship has brought us closer and closer together in all the experience of that feeling not like this. So I think the role of intimacy is the most sacred, transformative, transgressive, powerful, impactful gift and something that's alive. It's an organism that we care for and tend to because it's so profound. I think so many of us have felt the lack of true intimacy and the lack of not being seen or not feeling safe to be fully yourself and cared for and that being a process of growing together in, yes, feeling seen, but also feeling deeply cared for and thus able to see yourself in a new way. Like you make me want to step up and do the work of being my most present, my most dropped-in, my most stretching growing self in acts of care and seeing, but also in being held accountable and seeing the ways in which we call each other to grow. And that's incredibly intimate and vulnerable. These specific people (in the room) have been the most sacred thing in making sense of my life and my being, in the way that isn't always true in romantic partnerships, and when that is true, it's because I see that person as a friend first.

Ora: You brought up Mia's referring to the root of friendship being freedom, and in thinking about commitment, the commitment really is what allows for the trust, which allows for the feeling of safety, which allows for the growing and learning. Our queered model of and practice of friendship defies the way that freedom gets defined by whiteness and by capitalism, so the dominant culture that we're living in defines freedom as an island and that being free means being unaccountable and being able to do what-

ever you want. It's a definition of freedom that doesn't acknowledge interconnectivity and how our well-being
depends on each other's well-being and the well-being of all
plants and animals on the planet. So I think a beautiful
thing that queered friendship does is say that actually, we've
become more free in belonging to each other and in committing to each other so that we can do that growing and
healing. Especially now that we're getting our culture in the
mainstream a bit more, I do think it can be really enriching
and important for us to stay grounded in some of the political roots of queerness as this rejection of and building alternative ways of being to the white capitalist hetero-patriarchy.
So all of the things we've named that are so enriching for us
about our ways of being friends, like vulnerability, care, and
trust, are often devalued and often seen as "feminine,"
"weak," "gay"—but those are actually the things that make
us so strong! Being inspired by and getting to see your
friends as teachers, mentors, and comrades. And queering
friendship is also about infusing what we consider romance
and sensuality and seduction and flirtation, infusing that
into more than just one [romantic partner].

Gio: [screams] Yas! I was waiting for romance!

Ora: And the flip side is decentering the romantic partner—
not in a way that devalues—but I see all my relationships

including lovers as spokes in a hub. And that isolation that's created by the primary partner/nuclear family model that you were talking about, Sara Elise, is what is fed by making your romantic partner sometimes the only person or the person you're most committed to being intimate with, being vulnerable with, making life plans with, all of that. Thankfully, people are naming more the destructiveness of capitalism, but per usual, it's easier to critique the dominant system than it is to build alternatives and actually *live* alternatives. And I don't think we're ever going to truly dismantle and replace the current economic/political/social system we live in without actually queering friendships—which is queering community, which is creating these more liberatory and committed ways of being in relationships.

Sara Elise: *Yes.* Have y'all heard of Kate Johnson, a facilitator and activist? She put out a book this past year entitled *Radical Friendship.* She says that friendship has the possibility of strengthening community and movement spaces, and the act of committing to each other, staying together, and loving each other in our friendships help to build a stronger community, which helps to impact real change. And talks about our internalization of all of this external social messaging, like you brought up, Ora, which is all under white supremacy culture: policing, tendencies to isolate, individualism, vying for control and power . . .

Ora: Disposing of people . . .

Sara Elise: Exactly. The prioritization of yourself as an individual, which we think is what freedom is based on, but it's actually the thing that makes everyone weaker and thus less free. She talks about how it's possible to value ourselves and each other in a society where all of this external social messaging oftentimes manifests as our inner critic and self-doubt. So my next question is: How do we battle with all of this to get to a quality of friendship that helps that dominant system, and thus our inner critic, be less in charge?

Ora: Amen.

Sara Elise: We obviously can't get away from it in so many regards. We do create these mini utopias for ourselves, but ultimately, we're still functioning under this dominant system. But even if we can't get away from it, how do we move through it to actually connect in a way that's meaningful?

Naima: I don't have a fully formed thought yet, but touch feels very present to me and the ways that touch feels so central to the intimacy of our friendship. I find myself in moments wanting to hold you and squeeze you and love you and noticing how freeing that is to let things go that want to keep the body so separate. And in a friendship, your body is only shared with certain people and at certain times and in certain conditions. But I feel an impulse to rub and touch and kiss everyone all the time and that being part of our friendship.

Gio: I'm in therapy right now doing my own work and noticing where dominant systems are deeply entangled in my body and in my operating system. For me, one of those ways is just trying to present "keeping it all together" before I show up, and if I don't, I self-isolate or get very private. But in friendship, I think it's one of the places that's held me most accountable by naming it and feeling safe enough to know that that's my work here, and I think that comes from trust in everything we've built. And once that's there, I want to feel more free not being fully put together. I want to feel more free being ugly and emotional (or rather, what I regard as ugly and emotional, which I'm also working on undoing). But doing that here. Trust is required, and I think that's the work that's been done and will continue to be done. You know, we been in this, and I trust y'all. But naming it to you that that is my work is one way of undoing it, coming to you and saying to you, "This is something I'm working on," and even that is hard for me to do. But coming to you in process [anyway and getting better at] naming that it's ugly or hard without the capacity to clearly articulate something in the moment. Being in process and honoring the process is against the matrix of domination. And I think when [I] externalize something, it makes me feel more accountable, because I've shared it with someone and someone is privy to my work now.

Ora: Mm-hmm, that "witness" you were talking about.

Jessie: I recently listened again to the conversation between Esther Perel and Krista Tippett on eroticism. And eroticism as this powerful, transformative life force. And that eroticism is not sexual—it's like the shared joy of what it means to be alive together and the textural experiences of that life. Whether it be physical touch as one mode of how we express that, or feeding each other and the extreme sensual pleasure of eating a piece of meat or a fruit, or gifting each other with these sensory experiences as these tiny revolutionary celebrations of what it means to be alive together. And she said that people experience eroticism in physical expressions of revolution, like protest, so there's this whole incredible spectrum of erotic life force that I feel is so central to the way in which we love and care for each other and are present to life. Present to life as an antidote to death, which is these harmful structures of capitalism, white supremacy, patriarchy, all the things that have formed what we're taught to value or what we're taught that freedom is, or success, and how we think about ourselves as worthy or not or successful or not.

Ora: It's about abundance, too. We can infuse each other's lives and be our most generous and expansive selves when we're invited into it more constantly than just at these certain moments we're told, "This is who you do romance with." I am a big believer in flirtation. Because why wouldn't you want to make yourself and another person's every moment better? More playful? More energizing? And we do that for and with each other so we can have more of that. And that's also the positive side of some of the hard stuff that we might see as "ugly"—that when we take care of each other's egos, when we're feeding each other's egos and putting sugar in each other's bowls, then our egos are less ugly and they act out less. Humans are such social creatures because we're designed in our best form to be feeding each other. We see so much bad behavior in our society coming from these starved egos and empty bowls.

Sara Elise: Based on what you were saying about how romance or flirtation is reserved for certain relationships, I also wanted to explore how we view the differences between what we reserve for family versus friendship. Many people will reserve certain [moments] of "being seen" [only] for their family, like what Gio said: "My family can see me when I'm ugly and vulnerable, but maybe my friends can't." So I'm wondering how a friendship bond and a family bond differ to you. What's the line that separates the two for you? Or is there no line? What in your life is reserved for friendship versus what in your life is reserved just for family?

Naima: I think it's been the inverse for me, where my friends see more than my family does. And I've always felt that my friends know me more deeply. Family has always presented more internal struggle, and friendship has been really fortifying and nourishing. So yes, we're not blood related, but you are my family.

Ora: I think, Sara Elise, of a conversation we had on the train [several years ago]. It was one of the first times I fully understood the importance of our commitment to each other in terms of how you saw it as medicine and an opportunity to create something new and different for yourself from what your family of origin was for you. It makes me think that something about friends being family, and the queer definition of family that now even straight people are using—like, "Chosen family is a thing," and we're like, "Duh, that's literally how we [historically as queer people] have survived!" But if you break that down, it makes me think of boundaries and how in navigating the difference between our own needs and our family of origin's culture, or finding our place in it or taking care of ourselves within it, we're getting to wrestle with the worst stuff and teach each other the best stuff. And then creating something that allows us to evolve as humans. Ideally, then, as some of us are creating little humans, we're together literally collectively evolving by actually being able to process and build alternatives to help heal some of the wounds.

I come from a family where you'd never walk away and there's no isolation; in fact, isolation is not allowed. So in our exchange and our building together, Sara Elise, I'm able to transmute that to something that's helpful to you, and you can help me have better boundaries with them. So we're able to build family together and redefine what it means while healing those wounds, and learn from and inspire each other.

Jessie: I don't see a line between you and my blood family— it's just different branches of a tree of family. And I think that this being such a powerful space of healing has allowed me to start to do the work to end generational cycles of harm and violence [in my family]. I would not be able to make sense of that or to find the clarity or strength; I mean, you've all taught me so much about what it means to do that. It's like I speak a different language [with them]. And if I don't feel able to show up as my full authentic self, my past self would isolate. But because I feel held in the care [that I feel here] and feel the portals of access to that work, I'm able to be in presence with my blood family in a more intentional, loving, and compassionate way, because I know that they don't have this, and I have this. So I'm fortified. And I'm okay.

I can see my parents' hurt, and because they don't have this, they've never been able to do this work. So this has been really healing in the way I relate to my blood family because I have this, so I can bring that into my space with them—even if it's just a sense-making.

Naima: Portal is such a beautiful word, a great way to think about building friendship and family and what we're resourced by and what we have access to and how we can tap into each other for things we've never seen before or understood or had access to.

Ora: . . . And the commitment is healing. That's what stuck for me when we were [having that conversation] on the train—and Sara Elise and I have terrible memories. But it stuck in my brain, like, "Oh, this means something to her." And in that way, we were both transformed. Because then it was like, "Oh, my friendship is valuable to her." Because you said you noticed that I was willing to commit to you as much as my family. I wasn't prioritizing my blood family over our connection. In that way, I saw that was healing to you. And you articulated, "Wow, you really are about it," and that was so healing to me. It showed me my friendship is valuable.

Jessie: And it's deep, too, to see how with certain straight friends, I always feel like I'll be secondary to their romantic partnerships and to their blood family. So I always feel there's a limit, even if there's profound forever love and a feeling of sisterhood. I know that I'm loved and cared for by those people. But it's not the same. So I can't go there with them in the same way.

Ora: I like the imagery of the different branches on the same tree. I like thinking of it because the roots are about love, belonging, commitment—and [none of the branches is] more or less valuable.

Jessie: [Something that's always been messaged to me as I was growing up] was that friends come and go. You think now that your friendships are everything, but they're fleeting. And I've always deeply rejected that notion. So it's nice to know that we're all really committed, in it to win it.

Ora: And that the commitment is liberating! That's the deep thing.

Jessie: Yes, I want to keep building and folding even more life-making into that. There's no boundary between blood [family] and [what you mean to me].

Ora: And these are the fundamental building blocks of our lives, and as someone who just dismantled a romantic life-partner relationship, if these aren't the building blocks of our lives, we can say all the things we want in terms of criticizing the "matrix of domination," as Gio summarized it, but if the building blocks aren't different, then . . .

Sara Elise: We're just repeating the patterns.

Ora: Yes. What matters is how we're living our daily lives, because these are our building blocks! And if they're all about nuclear families and individual success or if it's very traditional heteronormative models of family . . . like for me, I think about all of that because it's become mostly clear that I'm not actually going to procreate, like myself with my body, and the way our society is set up is like—Who is going to take care of me? Literally. Because we don't have a social safety net, and we don't live in the kind of intergenerational communities in dominant culture. So for me, [our friendship] also helps me to not live in fear. And to make braver choices about who I am and what I want as a woman in the world, because it helps me feel like I'm not alone and that we're building something together that's not going to be predetermined by what was before.

Sara Elise: A queered friendship or a radical friendship isn't about a static thing, but it's something that's ever-changing. Practically, what goes into this daily work? What are the building blocks that you are referencing? What's the material that goes into queering your friendships?

Naima: Calling each other in during the moments where the impulse is to isolate or figure it out on our own. And then more on a visual level, the ways that we share pictures and videos and sounds and music and light, the things where we're saying "I don't actually have anything to verbally say to you right now, but I'm thinking of you and here's this picture." I send Jessie sounds all the time. Just thinking about how we can offer little delights even if there's no conversation around it. And also being okay with the distance and time sometimes in how frequently we might be able to communicate. The visual things and the sonic things for me sometimes are really important.

Ora: Definitely the sharing. If I were to go into list mode it would be: gifting, and not necessarily huge things, but the act of "I saw something and it made me think of you," or "I went to this place, and you were with me, and I'm bringing a piece of it back to you"; sharing what inspires us and what we learn from, which is almost how we ended up in this conversation; and I would add making plans in life—including each other in the decisions we're making about our lives. I think about it as "living life by committee." I always value the collective insight and think about decisions I make about what I'm doing in the world and how to live my life; those are decisions that I really benefit from [having] y'all's input on and perspective. And "if you feel something, say something," because you give the person the opportunity to tend to what you're feeling. And that's how you develop the trust that they want to tend to your feelings. And . . . butt squeezing.

The touch thing, I think, is part of the daily practice of it—to touch y'all. And flirt with you. And considering not [just thinking about] the concept of eroticism being expansive, but what is that [in practice]? Part of it is sharing delights and literally touching each other.

Sara Elise: Yes, yum. And lastly, do you have to be queer to queer your friendships?

Ora: I think you have to be queer to claim queerness. But if what we're saying is because we come from, as queer people, this incredible culture of spiritual and social genius born in the margins of a very violent and isolating society, that what we do hope for and need is everybody to unlearn those ways of being using processes and tools that they can honor, so that might mean needing to use different language, because queerness isn't theirs, but everyone needs to get free. It's tricky because in a queer world, not in the matrix of domination, there will be people who technically have certain anatomy that are attracted to each other or different genders that we typically call masculine and feminine that are attracted to each other, and that's not the point. Because in queerness, theoretically, there's room for all the attractions and the desires, including seeing everyone's capability of those changing along their life paths. However, we do have to be careful about language as we are living in the current system. So I do think it's tricky. How do we get from here to there in a way that isn't exploitative, or renders language that has been hard-fought and hard-wrought by people's lived experience less meaningful by anyone using it? But we don't want to deny them that freedom. But are they denying us ours if they're using language we've [had to fight] to exist?

Jessie: Yeah, we want to fold folks into these beautiful transformative, liberatory ways of being in the world. And also, as it is with any cultural appropriation, in what ways must that be deeply intentional and centering of legacies and histories of all the generations of all the folks who made our lives possible? And who made these ideas and ways accessible? How can we center history and queer history in these conversations so that the legacies don't get lost? So that it's not a disembodied thing that's just being appropriated and used without real intention and learning and unlearning and connection to where these ideas come from.

Ora: And something to consider is naming that you're trying to model that the way you're writing the chapter of this book. You're acknowledging that you're not an island, that these concepts are not new, you didn't craft them or create them yourself, that you're part of an ecosystem of relationships, and that you're learning and practicing with and through your people. This is what that looks like in practice—lifting up the names and stories and experiences that are a part of what I'm talking about.

It's interesting to see after many years that Octavia Butler and her body of work have started to move into the mainstream thanks to the hard work of many specifically Black queer feminist folks. And I think something I was thinking of while thinking of today's conversation specifically, and I'm certainly not the scholar that some of our other homies like Alexis or adrienne is, but over many years I've been impacted by her work. And one thing I think about with *Parable of the Sower*: one way that people have looked at that book is like, "Get ready, stay ready," and "Get your go pack," and that's all very true, because we need that to make sure we're surviving and self-determining. But what I've always found so powerful in *Parable of the Sower* is that for Olamina, yes, it's important she learns how to shoot a gun and seed save, but actually as a small Black girl making it in an apocalyptic world, to me what is so clearly her most valuable survival skill is being able to cultivate relationships of trust and loyalty. That's how she doesn't get killed and that's how she ends up actually creating a whole community of her own. And that's something I think about all the time: that these are survival skills, being able to nurture these relationships. I'm somebody who doesn't have a lot of material wealth, but I'm always rich in friendships, and these relationships are my greatest currency. And I think that's true for everyone, but we live in a society that underestimates and devalues and invisibilizes how much relationships are how anything gets done and how we make it at all.

Naima: I also think that so much of this conversation is about making plain the labor it takes to get to a place like that. And not making that work invisible either. I think when I first heard that question, I immediately said yes, and I think what I was saying yes to was to not make that labor invisible and to not cosplay as queer without doing the work of understanding how we got to this place. So I do agree to, yes, folding people in and seeing the beauty of how we get to a place like this, but also to not just jump in and say, "Oh, I'm queering my friendship now," without understanding the time and the work it takes to do that.

Ora: We're pushing back and going back and forth between romance and effort, delight and work. And that actually counters how these things get defined. Like "romance isn't supposed to have work" or "friendship isn't supposed to have work," because if we get to a place where they need work, they're out.

Jessie: And also a sidebar, too: [it's important to note] that many gay people are not moving from a place of queer legacy and queer values and queer histories and are just replicating heteronormative ways of being in the world and valuing certain things over collective being. So it's not about who you're having sex with, but it's about a way of being in the world—a politic, a practice . . .

Sara Elise: . . . And honoring the legacy of these folks who've been living and creating and surviving in these alternative systems all along.

Ora: And there is the honoring of the legacy, but also there's risk involved. It's not just about honoring the history and reading the books, which are important, but are you going to take the risk? Are you going to say you're queering your friendship, but you're not going to let yourself be vulnerable in certain ways, like saying, "Hey, I want to build a life with you, my friend," which is taking a risk with rejection and not having a clear road map of how you do that. Some of that work that Naima's talking about is, Are you going to take the risk that queer people have and have had to do in order to build something differently?

GRATITUDE

I composed this chapter with inexpressible appreciation at the forefront of my mind and heart, especially for my closest friends and family. Though not all of you were physically present for this particular conversation, your support, laughter, sharing, tenderness, and warm community have provided a safe container so that I might have the room to grow up and into my self, thus providing the incomparable gift of learning myself more fully as we've grown in our friendship together.

ORA WISE (she/her) is a queer chef and cultural producer based in Brooklyn, New York. She is cofounder of FIG, a grassroots collective developing community food webs that build health, wealth, and solidarity. Wise is the creator of Radical Hospitality, a multimedia project exploring practices embodying generosity, care, connection, and creativity as essential to the social transformation needed as we resist war, authoritarianism, and climate destruction. She can be found at @orawise.

JESSIE LEVANDOV (she/her) is an award-winning filmmaker, visual artist, and educator based in Brooklyn, New York. Jessie directed community filmmaking programs in New York City public schools, arts organizations, and community spaces for more than a decade. In 2018, she cofounded Mala Forever, a production company and creative and editorial studio based in New York and Los Angeles. You can follow her at @jessielevandov.

NAIMA GREEN (she/her) is at first a lover and a lover at last. Between those points are pictures and even sonic. Beneath those pictures and even sonic are dreams and spit containing a want. Naima Green carries the want inside her throat and drips it out with a lens. Often, light. As an artist, she senses. As a sensualist, she's made. You can find her at @naimagreen.

GIOVANNA FISCHER (she/her) is an educator and cultural strategist based in Los Angeles. She centers teaching and learning in the design of systems and experiences that nurture creativity and support inclusive cultural production. Her work encompasses fifteen years of teaching, facilitating, and leading learning projects and programs. She can be found at @giofisch.

Roasted Squash and Garlic Ricotta Buckwheat Galette Recipe

I created this recipe in response to a desire to share something comforting and delicious with my friends who have a variety of dietary restrictions and allergies. I wanted us to feel satiated but not tired, so that we would have energy for our dialogue. I made the crust using buckwheat flour so that it would be easier to digest, a better option for the less gluten-tolerant of our group. I incorporated roasted garlic into the local ricotta to provide a depth of flavor, and I incorporated herbs into the roasted squash to provide some brightness to the seasonal ingredients. The galette was easy to make and well received, so I am sharing it here for you to enjoy with the people you love.

GALETTE DOUGH

1 cup buckwheat flour

¾ cup unbleached all-purpose flour

1 teaspoon fresh thyme leaves

½ cup (1 stick) butter, chilled and cut into cubes

5 tablespoons ice water, as needed

1 whole egg, beaten, for egg wash

Sprinkle of Maldon Sea Salt Flakes

FILLING

2–3 tablespoons extra-virgin olive oil

3 cups cubed butternut squash (¼–½ inch cubes)

2 teaspoons fresh thyme

1 garlic clove, minced

1 whole egg

1 cup fresh, local ricotta
(Hint: Don't skimp on the quality of this ingredient! It really makes a huge difference if you can get the good stuff.)

4 garlic cloves, roasted
(Hint: Throw the entire garlic head in the oven with some olive oil and roast the full head. You can use whatever you don't need for this recipe on other things you make throughout the week.)

¼–½ cup gruyere, grated

Sea salt and ground black pepper, to taste

MAKE THE DOUGH

Add both flours, the salt, and the thyme leaves to a food processor (or a large mixing bowl) and pulse to combine. Add in the cubes of cold butter and pulse or mix together with your hands until pea-size chunks form. Add the cold water, 1 tablespoon at a time, until a shaggy dough forms. Pull out the dough and form it into a flat disk. Wrap it in plastic wrap and chill in the fridge for 30 minutes (or make the dough the day before and chill it overnight).

MAKE THE SQUASH FILLING

Toss the cubed squash and the minced garlic, sea salt, black pepper, fresh thyme, and olive oil together in a mixing bowl. Make sure to thoroughly coat the ingredients in olive oil so they don't burn while roasting. Spread in an even layer on a rimmed baking sheet and roast 20–30 minutes, until the squash browns. Remove from the oven and let cool thoroughly before adding to the galette.

MAKE THE RICOTTA FILLING

Mix the roasted garlic cloves in with the ricotta, 1 tablespoon of olive oil, sea salt, and black pepper to taste.

ASSEMBLE THE GALETTE

Preheat your oven to 425 degrees. Lightly sprinkle flour on your countertop and unwrap your dough disk. Roll it out into a flattened (¼-inch thick), 12-inch circle. Move the dough circle to a parchment-lined baking sheet to begin assembly.

Smear the garlic ricotta filling into the center of the dough, around 1–2 inches from the edge, in an even application. Put the roasted squash on top of the garlic ricotta, making sure to pour any oil from the pan on top.

Gently fold your dough edges over and back into the center, forming a round galette shape. If any of the crust breaks, just pinch it together with a bit of water on your fingers. Brush the assembled galette crust with egg yolk. Sprinkle the whole galette with the grated gruyere and sprinkle the flaky Maldon salt on the crust.

BAKE YOUR GALETTE

Bake for 30–45 minutes depending on your oven (you can start checking after 30 minutes and bake until the dough is golden brown).

Once the galette is baked, remove from the oven and let cool for 10 minutes before slicing like a pie and serving to your loved ones.

Let the Energy of the World Support You

When I choose to see the good side of things, I'm not being naive. It is strategic and necessary. It's how I've learned to survive through everything.

—WAYMOND WANG,
EVERYTHING EVERYWHERE ALL AT ONCE

THIS BOOK IS FOR PEOPLE WHO WANT TO SEE THE GOODNESS, WHO want to be soft in the face of hardness, who want to let their softness touch others. And some days, it might not feel possible. Some days, it's difficult for me to live by the words that I've shared with you. I am certainly not able to access my highest self every day, and I accept that that's okay. Throughout the process of writing this book, I have experienced immeasurable loss and heartache. In addition to living through the ongoing COVID pandemic, I lost my cousin and my uncle in a violent murder, and my uncle was one of the sweetest and most supportive humans I've ever had the privilege of knowing. I lost my emotional support dog, with whom I shared a deeply special understanding. My wife was also diagnosed with terminal breast and bone cancer in the midst of our separation, after an immensely beautiful nine-year codependent relationship. We met at a coffee shop and decided that we officially needed space to end things, and I cried in bed for hours (and then again for many more hours in the year that followed).

It's important to allow people to change and to know when to reevaluate your path together, to know when a blessing is no longer for you. Even though I knew this was the best decision for both of us, I felt so unsure about how to move forward after almost a decade of building a life together with her. Later that evening, another partner of mine invited me to go to a jazz show in a brownstone in my neighborhood, right down the street. Apparently, BrownstoneJAZZ had been around for the past nine years, though I had never experienced it. Even though I felt tender and antisocial, we wound up going, and something opened in me. The music swept me away in sensory bliss, and in that moment I felt fully present, separate from my fear of what might happen next with my wife, separate from my yearning for and grieving of what we used to be. I felt fully held and present to the moments unfurling around me, my everchangingly new life unraveling and expanding within me, and the energy of the world providing exactly what I needed in the time that I needed it most. That evening, I spontaneously heard a jazz show with some of Brooklyn's biggest jazz players (some who had flown in specifically for that one particular show) in one of the most historically significant places to the 1970s and 1980s jazz revolution. And I learned the lesson that I have learned before and am excited to learn again and again into forever: when you let yourself be moved intuitively, Spirit/God/The Universe (however you revere and identify this energy) tends to show up for you at the most unexpected and needed times.

The Earth is built in counterbalance, and all energy in the world follows this pattern: a balance of light and dark, rooting and rising, moments of deep pain and lighthearted revelry, growing in life and decaying into death. Neither is bad or good, and without one end of the spectrum, we don't have the other. This book is about paying attention, following your intuitive knowing, and creating space for the "more"—for shifting into position to actively manifest and receive abundance. But in order to create room for the "more" in your life, you have to first identify your "less."

I took a womb workshop with healer Lana Homeri in 2019 where we talked about moving out stagnant energy to create space in our bodies and minds to allow for life's juiciness and abundance to flow in effortlessly. And what a concept! So that

New Year's Eve, and then each year after that, I wrote down my "less" and "more" list. I first got the idea of this list from Daryl Nuhn—a lovely human, fellow silly Gemini, and co-owner of New York's Peoples Wine and Prima—and used that inspiration to create my annual "Releasing for the Juiciness" exercise, which I share annually on social media. Since then, hundreds of people from all over the world have sent me their #Releasing fortheJuiciness "less/more" lists.

So where in your life are you looking to release? What are you holding onto that's taking up space and thus energy, effort, prioritization, and focus that can all be potentially directed elsewhere? We first have to know what we need to say no to, what we should have more firm boundaries around, what we need to release, in order to create a foundation for ourselves to say yes, allowing refreshed energy and new opportunities to flow into our lives.

My most recent list looked like this:

Less (moving stagnant energy out . . .)

Upper limiting or "too good to be true" thinking

Finding reasons to talk myself out of things

Negative self-talk

Questioning (myself) and comparing (to others)

Masking when there's an opportunity to let down my mask safely

Rushing to get to a destination (physically, mentally)

Trying to control the flow

Overexplaining or defending myself to be likable or feel understood

Glorification of "other"

Computer-based activities and hobbies

More (. . . to bring in the juiciness of life)

Finding the woo and romance in the everyday

Doing the first thought that pops in my mind

Affirmation of myself in the present moment

Stretching

Slow-cooked meals

Doing the weirdest possible thing

Purchasing (and making) art

Financial abundance

Learning from plants, herbs, fungi (the Earth)

Slowness, presence, deep breaths

Recognizing that new physical health needs provide opportunities for learning and deepening in my relationship to self

Learning more about my autism and being vocal (and satisfied) with the way I experience the world

In order to let the energy of the world support you, you have to first make space internally for it to support you. And then when the space is there, you have to actually accept the energetic support you're receiving. We must remind ourselves that we are here changing, made of the same form that the Earth is made of, and that just as the flow of energy supports the Earth and the Earth knows what to do, the flow of energy is also here to support our life path as well.

This past year when I was looking for a new place to live on my own for the first time ever in my life (which is a huge deal especially because of my autistic needs), I sent out an email asking friends whether they had any leads or knew of any options. My close friend J responded almost immediately to my apartment hunt question and, in the voice note they left me, said, "I also wrote back really quickly too because it's just nice to know that when you ask, you will be received. That there are always options, you know?" That, to me, feels like abundance. Knowing that when there's uncertainty, if I ask for support, I will be received and cared for in this request. There's always room for change, responsiveness from my community, resources to take advantage of. *There are always options.*

Perhaps Geminis are known as being indecisive because each choice to us feels as though it carries the weight of losing all the rest. There's a nostalgia I feel even before I say goodbye that feels heavy and makes me so sad that sometimes I'll cry before a choice has even been made, until I'm sinking into the depths of my present choice feeling overjoyed and drowning in how good it feels. Still, I remember always what I have lost, what I've said no to in order to make room for this choice. The overthinking never stops. It can pause, yes, in moments of embodiment and presence. But it never stops. "The mind is maya" is a Hindu concept that describes the instability of our mind and its ever-changing thoughts and emotional states. Sri Ramana Maharshi, a Hindu spiritual leader, once said, "Reality lies beyond the mind. So long as the mind functions, there is duality, maya, etc. Only once it is transcended, can the reality shine forth."

And still, we are here. So what can we do with that? How do we quiet our minds even despite the ever-present hum of our impending destruction? In the 2022 film *You Won't Be Alone*, the narrator shares "It's a burning, breaking thing, this world, a biting, retching thing. And yet . . . and yet . . . I am a man now. And so I can do it. Go out where the grass is. Where the soil is. Clothe myself in sun."

How do we contemplate *in our bodies* the divinity of our bittersweet, and sometimes horrific, shared experience? And what can we make of our experienced and present life, this immense and wondrous gift?

T Wise, one of my closest friends and a brilliant storyteller, once shared this poem/scripture:

I have to try
every day
to be kind to myself
to understand what others need
to let go of what keeps me stagnant
to be sensible and sensitive
everything we love is woven with loss
we pick at the wool of it and wonder
how then, to make from these days
a festival and not a funeral
small steps
small stones
small lives
but each one a whole world
in a small home
filled with first green and spice and smooth stones
praise to the small things
we want to be held
and we don't need to act
like we don't

Thank you.

ACKNOWLEDGMENTS

To the land we're on—this Earth and her medicine—the air we breathe, the fire we harness to nourish and create, water, sky, the humbling Moon: thank you to the nonhuman forces, for your powerful and protective presence. Thank you to God/Spirit/Source, the energy and power to which I have always, and will always, belong. To the people who steward and protect the land, who work tirelessly for all of us so that our future can look different than it does right now, I thank you and honor you.

The most profound gratitude is for my daily care team and the healers + practitioners I work with each month: your service empowers me to accomplish a great deal more than I could on my own. In the deep waters of my mind, you anchor me to this world. Your care is what facilitates my daydreaming. You enable my living, and without that gift—none of this would be possible. Thank you for showing up and showing me (through your actions) that my needs are not a burden. Thank you for ensuring that I am never alone when I need help.

Thank you to my Uncle Eric and Aunt Connie, my grandparents (especially Grandad, Grandmom, and Gami), and other relatives for loving me and doing the best that you know how to do. Thank you to my old and new ancestors.

Thank you to my parents for the protected container of childhood you worked dutifully to make possible so that I had ample time for solitude and imagination. Thank you Daddy for raising me to be a critical thinker and for teaching me how to play the game. Thank you Mommy for your unashamed wonder, your tenderness of heart and sensitivity to the world that is my most valuable inheritance.

Thank you to my little lanterns: my brother Jake, for being my earliest (and most annoying) cheerleader. And my sisters Lily and Sofi for teaching me sage lessons about visibility, self-expression, and rebellion. And thank you to my newest siblings: Jordy + Sabrina: my life has more love with you in it.

It has taken numerous people to usher *A Recipe for More* into readers' hands, and my appreciation goes out to each one of you. To Yin who suggested I cater and speak at an event in Brooklyn whereupon I met the fierce Judith, who is the person who asked me if I ever considered writing a book and offered me this opportunity (and is one of my biggest advocates)—thank you.

To the contributors, composers, and artists I leaned on while in the process of this book's creation, whose work helped inspire this one—thank you. And to adrienne maree brown for reminding me that "my heart work is not a burden, but a gift." Thank you to india arie's 2001 album, *Acoustic Soul*, for igniting my manifestation habits early. Thank you to small bookstores, warm and nurturing portals to our biggest dreamwork.

To everyone who picks up *A Recipe for More* at some point over the course of your lifetime, conjuring a future of gushing abundance—thank you. Even though we're all no more (or less) than stardust—for this moment, at this time, in this reality, the things I write about feel like they matter. (Ultimately they don't, of course. None of it does. It's all an illusion.) Thank you for trusting me with your time. Thank you to the young people for teaching us all how to imagine, play, trust, and rest—how to do the big work.

Thank you to the Black readers, the Indigenous readers, the autistic readers, the femmes, the leatherdykes, the introverts, the queerdos and the weirdos—we are on this journey together. I wrote this for us.

To Cristine, thank you for your never-ending support and spoiling of me.

To my community—you know who you are. Thank you for being both my peers and my teachers. Thank you for your commitment to our shared life together that enriches us all.

And finally, to my Twin Flame—you help me hold my heart. Your reflective companionship, unwavering devotion, (fatherly) belief in me, grounding insights and suggestions, and you yourself made this book (and my life's continual expansion over the past fifteen years) possible. Thank you.

with abounding gratitude and love,
sara elise
November 2024

REFERENCES

Ackerman, Diane. *A Natural History of the Senses*. London: Phoenix, 1996.

Alphachanneling. *Book of the Utopian Erotic*. Oakland, CA: Flowering Drum, 2018.

"American Revolutionary: On Revolution at Berkeley." Excerpts of a conversation between Grace Lee Boggs and Angela Davis at the University of California, Berkeley, 2012. *POV*, season 27, episode 2, aired June 29, 2014. PBS North Carolina. Video. video.pbsnc.org/video/pov-american-revolutionary-revolution-berkeley/.

Bass, Ellen. "The Thing Is." *Poetry of Presence: An Anthology of Mindfulness Poems*. West Hartford, CT: Grayson Books, 2017. Reprinted, *Poetry Foundation*, www.poetryfoundation.org/poems/151844/the-thing-is.

Birdsong, Mia. *How We Show Up: Building Community in These Fractured Times*. New York: Hachette Books, 2020.

Black Disabled Creatives, blackdisabledcreatives.com/.

Botton, Alain De. "On Learning to Live Deeply Rather than Broadly." *The School of Life*, January 13, 2021. www.theschooloflife.com/thebookoflife/on-living-deeply-rather-than-lengthily/.

Brach, Tara. "Tara Brach on Embodied Presence (Part 1): Planting Our Roots in the Universe." *TarahBrach.com*, January 22, 2020. https://www.tarabrach.com/embodied-presence-part-1/.

Bridgforth, Sharon. "Dat Black Mermaid Man Lady: Dem Blessings." Made possible by the Doris Duke Performing Artist Awards program, the Whitman Institute, Thousand Currents Artist In-Residence Program, with development support from New Dramatists Creativity Fund (a program made possible by a generous grant from the Andrew W. Mellon Foundation); a project of Creative Capital. Video. 2020.

brown, adrienne maree. "Murmurations: Love Looks Like Accountability." *Yes Magazine*, July 25, 2022. https://www.yesmagazine.org/opinion/2022/07/25/love-accountability-adrienne-maree-brown.

———— . *Pleasure Activism: The Politics of Feeling Good.* Chico, CA: AK Press, 2019.

Brown, Brene. *Dare to Lead.* London: Vermilion, 2018.

Chopra, Deepak. *Metahuman.* London: Penguin Random House, 2020.

Christiansen, Richard. "Flamingo Estate: Do you know about real hospitality?" Instagram, September 20, 2022. https://www.instagram.com/p/CiuqrtfP5Io/.

Collins English Dictionary. Accessed December 6, 2022. http://www.collinsdictionary.com/english.

Dispenza, Joe. *Evolve Your Brain: The Science of Changing Your Mind.* Deerfield Beach, FL: Health Communications, 2008.

Emezi, Akwaeke. *Pet.* New York: Make Me a World, 2019.

Everything Everywhere All at Once, dir. Daniel Kwan and Daniel Scheinert. New York: A24, 2022.

Green, Misha, et al., screenwriters. *Lovecraft Country.* Season 1, episode 7, "I Am." Based on *Lovecraft Country* by Matt Ruff. Aired October 18, 2020, on HBO.

Gumbs, Alexis Pauline. Undrowned: Black Feminist Lessons from Marine Mammals. Chico, CA: AK Press, 2020.

Hale, Kori. "The $300 Billion Black American Consumerism Bag Breeds Big Business Opportunities." *Forbes,* September 17, 2021. https://www.forbes.com/sites/korihale/2021/09/17/the-300-billion-black-american-consumerism-bag-breeds-big-business-opportunities.

Hall, Steph Barron. "Nine Types of Rest." *Nine Types,* December 26, 2019. https://ninetypes.co/blog/nine-types-of-rest.

Hart, Julia (director and writer), and Jordan Horowitz (writer). *Fast Color.* Universal City, CA: Codeblack Films, 2018 (US release: April 19, 2019).

Headlee, Celeste Anne. *Do Nothing: How to Break Away from Overworking, Overdoing, and Underliving.* New York: Harmony Books, 2020.

Hendricks, Gay. *The Big Leap: Conquer Your Hidden Fear and Take Life to the Next Level.* New York: HarperCollins, 2010.

Hersey, Tricia. "Resting on and for the Earth," interview by Brontë Velez. *Atmos,* April 28, 2021. https://atmos.earth/rest-resistance-colonization-black-liberation/.

hooks, bell. "bell hooks and Laverne Cox in a Public Dialogue at The New School." YouTube video, October 13, 2014.

hooks, bell, and Thich Nhat Hanh. "Building a Community of Love: bell hooks and Thich Nhat Hanh." *Lion's Roar*, March 24, 2017. https://www .lionsroar.com/bell-hooks-and-thich-nhat-hanh-on-building-a-com munity-of-love/.

"Jason Reynolds: Imagination and Fortitude." *On Being with Krista Tippett*, June 25, 2020. Podcast. https://onbeing.org/programs/jason-reynolds -imagination-and-fortitude/.

Johnson, Kate. *Radical Friendship*. Boulder, CO: Shambhala, 2021.

Jones, Luvvie Ajayi. "Get Comfortable with Being Uncomfortable." TED video, January 2, 2018. https://www.youtube.com/watch?v=QijH4UA qGD8.

Kimmerer, Robin Wall. *Braiding Sweetgrass*. Minneapolis: Milkweed Editions, 2015.

Lally, Phillippa, Cornelia H. M. van Jaarsveld, Henry W. W. Potts, and Jane Wardle. "How Are Habits Formed: Modelling Habit Formation in the Real World." *European Journal of Social Psychology* 40, no. 6 (2009): 998– 1009. https://onlinelibrary.wiley.com/doi/abs/10.1002/ejsp.674.

Lelio, Sebastián (director and writer), and Rebecca Leniewicz (writer). *Disobedience*. London: Film4 Productions and FilmNation Entertainment, 2017. Based on the novel *Disobedience* by Naomi Alderman.

Live from Snack Time. "How About I Take a Nap for a Treat?" Twitter, April 29, 2020. https://twitter.com/livefromsnackti/status/12556579634 33287687.

Lockley, Alisha. "The Anatomy of Intimacy." TEDxFSCJ video. Filmed May 7, 2015, at Florida State College at Jacksonville. https://www.you tube.com/watch?v=A3yBxsDv8lM.

Lorde, Audre. *The Black Unicorn: Poems*. New York: W. W. Norton & Company, 1995. Originally published 1978.

———. "Learning from the 60s" (speech), Harvard University, February 1982. *Blackpast*. www.blackpast.org/african-american-history/1982-audre -lorde-learning-60s/.

———. "Uses of the Erotic: The Erotic as Power." Paper presented at the Fourth Berkshire Conference on the History of Women, Mount Holyoke

College, South Hadley, MA, August 25, 1978. Published as a pamphlet by Out & Out Books (available from Crossing Press) and reprinted in *Sister Outsider: Essays and Speeches by Audre Lorde* (Berkeley, CA: Crossing Press, 1984).

"Maxine Hong Kingston on Imagination and Writing: Part 2." *BillMoyers .com*, March 4, 1990. billmoyers.com/content/maxine-hong-kingston -part-2/.

May, Katherine. *Wintering: The Power of Rest and Retreat in Difficult Times.* London: Rider, 2020.

Mills, Paul J., Christine Tara Peterson, Meredith A. Pung, Sheila Patel, Lizabeth Weiss, Kathleen L. Wilson, P. Murali Doraiswamy, Jeffery A. Martin, Rudolph E. Tanzi, and Deepak Chopra. "Change in Sense of Non-dual Awareness and Spiritual Awakening in Response to a Multidimensional Well-Being Program." *Journal of Alternative and Complementary Medicine* 24, no. 4 (April 1, 2018). https://35s3f14rw1s1sr3rc1nk656ib9 -wpengine.netdna-ssl.com/wp-content/uploads/2017/11/SBTI-nondual -manuscript-JACM.pdf.

Ngangura, Tarisai. "A Portrait of a Black Woman in Kink." *Playboy*, February 19, 2020. www.playboy.com/read/black-bondage.

Nin, Anaïs. *The Diary of Anaïs Nin*, ed. Gunther Stuhlmann. New York: Swallow Press, 1966.

Pang, Camilla. *Explaining Humans: What Science Can Teach Us About Life, Love and Relationships.* New York: Penguin, 2021.

Parker, Priya. *Art of Gathering: Creating Breakthrough Spaces That Transform the Ways We Live, Love, Learn and Lead.* New York: Penguin, 2018.

Perel, Esther. "Are We Asking Too Much of Our Spouses?" *TED Radio Hour*, April 25, 2014. National Public Radio. https://www.npr.org/tran scripts/301825600.

———. "Episode 2: Sex Work: The Unofficial Resume." *How's Work*, n.d. Podcast. howswork.estherperel.com/episodes/episode-2.

Petersen, Anne Helen. "How Millennials Became the Burnout Generation." *BuzzFeed News*, January 5, 2019. www.buzzfeednews.com/article /annehelenpetersen/millennials-burnout-generation-debt-work.

Plum Village. "How to Let Anger Out: Thich Nhat Hanh Answers Questions." YouTube video. January 17, 2015. www.youtube.com/watch?v=W TF9xgqLIvI.

Portinari, Folco. "The Slow Food Manifesto." Slow Food USA, December 10, 1989. https://slowfoodusa.org/manifesto/.

Powell, Neesha. "3 Ways To Decolonize Your Nonprofit as Told by a Black Queer Feminist Organizer." *Everyday Feminism*, May 14, 2018. everyday feminism.com/2018/05/decolonizing-nonprofits/.

"Resmaa Menakem: 'Notice the Rage; Notice the Silence.'" *On Being with Krista Tippett*, November 8, 2021. Podcast. onbeing.org/programs/resmaa -menakem-notice-the-rage-notice-the-silence/.

Róisín, Fariha. *Who Is Wellness For?* New York: HarperCollins, 2022.

"Ross Gay: Tending Joy and Practicing Delight." *On Being with Krista Tippett*, July 25, 2019. Podcast. onbeing.org/programs/ross-gay-tending-joy -and-practicing-delight/.

Sadagat, Ica. "letter to julia: on joy." *IcaSadagat.co*. December 1, 2020. https://us17.campaign-archive.com/?u=9410b698c0fadc8c8396015 cc&id=dfeacef536.

Sasaki, Fumio. *Goodbye, Things: The New Japanese Minimalism*. New York: W. W. Norton & Company, 2017.

Schmidt, Amy. "Abundance." *Rattle*, January 20, 2019. www.rattle.com /abundance-by-amy-schmidt/.

Selassie, Sebene. *The Call for Connection: A Free Moonly Newsletter*, January 2022. https://www.sebeneselassie.com/thecall.

———. *You Belong: A Call for Connection*. New York: HarperCollins, 2020.

Sri Ramana Maharshi. "Talk 433" (December 26, 1937). In *Talks with Sri Ramana Maharshi*. Tiruvannamalai, Tamil Nadu, India: Sri Ramanasramam, 2003.

Stewart, Danté. "Black Rage in an Anti-Black World Is a Spiritual Virtue." *Sojourners*, May 29, 2020. sojo.net/articles/black-rage-anti-black-world -spiritual-virtue.

Swart, Tara. "The 4 Underlying Principles of Changing Your Brain." *Forbes*, March 27, 2018. www.forbes.com/sites/taraswart/2018/03/27/the -4-underlying-principles-to-changing-your-brain/?sh=750382935a71.

Tosi, Christina. *Dessert Can Save the World: Stories, Secrets, and Recipes for a Stubbornly Joyful Existence*. New York: Harmony Books, 2022.

Vasudev, Jaggi. *Karma: A Yogi's Guide to Crafting Your Destiny.* New York: Penguin, 2021.

Vaughn, Mikeisha Dache. "Rest as Resistance: Why Nap Ministry and Others Want Black People to Sleep." *Complex*, May 7, 2021. www.complex.com/life/black-power-naps-rest-as-resistance.

Vaynerchuk, Gary. "You Care Too Much About Other People's Opinions." YouTube video. April 7, 2022. https://www.youtube.com/watch?v=u-dNSxgy8LY.

Washington Post Live. "Transcript: Race in America: Giving Voice with Jason Reynolds." *The Washington Post*, February 24, 2022. www.washingtonpost.com/washington-post-live/2022/02/24/transcript-race-america-giving-voice-with-jason-reynolds/.

Woke Kindergarten. Home page, n.d. Accessed September 20, 2022. https://www.wokekindergarten.org.

Zimmer, Eric. *The One You Feed*, December 16, 2022. Podcast.

SARA ELISE is a community cultivator and interdisciplinary creative, splitting her time between Brooklyn and The Catskills, New York. She is the cofounder + designer of Apogeo Collective, a hospitality collective centering the experiences of Queer and Trans People of Color, with an internationally based flagship hotel concept space (Apogeo Guest House). She is also the founder of Harvest & Revel, a Brooklyn-based event catering + production company that pioneered the sustainable-food movement over a decade ago and now works with clients like Louis Vuitton House, Carnegie Mellon Foundation, Instagram, and Nike.

She recently designed and opened Again Vintage, a homewares shop and cafe space in Brooklyn that bridges the connection between community, design, gut-healing food + beverage, slowness + ritual, and celebrating home as sanctuary.

Sara Elise has been featured in *Dazed*, *Autostraddle*, *Playboy*, *Interview Magazine*, *Essence*, *Afropunk*, *Healthyish*, *Well + Good*, *Nylon*, *StyleLikeU*, and *them*, among other publications.

As an autistic Black & Indigenous femme, she spends much of her thoughtspace contemplating pleasure + pain, collective joy, otherness, embodiment, remembering + reclaiming, self-destruction, and growth—and how inextricably those concepts are linked. To that end, Sara Elise has deep interests in ritualization, BDSM, relationship dynamics, and the development of decolonized personal awareness and well-being. With all of her work, she aims to challenge our collective reality by first reimagining and then creating alternative systems and spaces for her communities to thrive. You can join her community-making at @SaraElise333 on Instagram, and find more of her writing at saraelise.substack.com.